How to Snog a Hagfish!
Disgusting Things in the Sea

Jonathan Eyers

E
D0994113
30

For Simon Levitas and Steve Whittle

By the same author
Don't Shoot the Albatross! – Nautical Myths and Superstitions

Published by Adlard Coles Nautical
an imprint of Bloomsbury Publishing Plc
50 Bedford Square, London WC1B 3DP
www.adlardcoles.com

Copyright © Jonathan Eyers 2012

First edition published 2012

ISBN 978-1-4081-4042-0

All rights reserved. No part of this publication may be reproduced in any form
or by any means – graphic, electronic or mechanical, including photocopying,
recording, taping or information storage and retrieval systems – without the
prior permission in writing of the publishers.

The right of the author to be identified as the author of this work has
been asserted by him in accordance with the Copyright, Designs and
Patents Act, 1988.

A CIP catalogue record for this book is available from the British Library.

This book is produced using paper that is made from wood grown in managed,
sustainable forests. It is natural, renewable and recyclable. The logging and
manufacturing processes conform to the environmental regulations of the
country of origin.

Typeset in Haarlemmer MT 10pt on 12pt
Printed and bound in India by Replika Press Pvt Ltd

Note: while all reasonable care has been taken in the publication of this
book, the publisher takes no responsibility for the use of the methods or
products described in the book.

CONTENTS

PHOTO CREDITS

Most of the images in this book are reproduced with the kind permission of the National Oceanic and Atmospheric Administration (NOAA). You can learn more about their mission (and see more photos from their library) on their website: www.noaa.gov

Images credited to individual photographers are used under the Creative Commons license: http://creativecommons.org/licenses/by/3.0

Eric Charlton: 67; Getty Images: 45; Rex Features: 6.

Note: To the best of the publisher's knowledge, unless specified otherwise all the images herein are public domain and have been designated as such by the copyright holder. Should an image have been used without being credited to the proper copyright holder the publisher is happy to amend this for any future reprinting.

Introduction
BENEATH THE SURFACE...

For many people, seasickness is the most unpleasant thing that happens to them at sea. Beneath the surface of the sea, however, is a whole other world, a lot of which could turn all but the strongest stomachs.

But disgust is actually pretty irrational, when you think about it. Someone who is disgusted when they see a dead bird lying by the side of the road can perfectly happily drive home and eat another dead bird for dinner.

Once upon a time, before the days of 'best before' or 'use by' dates, we relied on our own senses to tell us when food was good to eat. Disgust is a primitive defence mechanism designed to make us avoid bad food before we put it in our mouths – or to vomit it back up if it's already too late.

Feelings of disgust come from the primal part of the brain that warns us of danger, even when the logical side of our brain tells us there's nothing to be worried about. In this way, disgust is nowadays about as rational as any other phobia.

You probably wouldn't want to eat many of the species featured in *How to Snog a Hagfish!*, but plenty of people around the world do! Reading this book might not make you want to join them, but understanding how and why these amazing creatures have developed the way they have may make them seem just a little less disgusting. Or of course it may not.

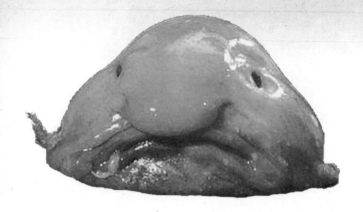

Chapter 1
LOOKS AREN'T EVERYTHING

If you are a fish the size of a pencil in an ocean full of sharks the size of trucks, you probably shouldn't expect to die of old age. If you are lucky, you were born with the ability to defend yourself, preferably with poison (see page 36) or electricity (see page 40). If you are unlucky, you might have to rely on your appearance, and hope other creatures in the sea think you look distinctly unappetising.

Many people consider the **Blobfish** to be the ugliest creature in the sea. Indeed, Blobfish is an appropriate name for an animal that consists mainly of a jellylike substance. It has hardly any muscles and can't really swim. Instead, it just floats about wherever the currents take it, buoyed up by its jelly body, which has a similar density to seawater. Of course, not being able to swim very far, it can't hunt for food either. So it just eats whatever drifts past, from small molluscs to smaller fish. Fortunately for the Blobfish, just floating about doesn't use up much energy, so it doesn't need to eat much either.

Living off the coast of Australia at depths of about 2,600ft (800m), the Blobfish is rarely seen by humans. When caught in a fishing net and brought to the surface, the Blobfish quickly dries out in the air – and pops. It makes quite a mess. But perhaps the real reason we find it so disgusting is because, looking at it head on, the Blobfish bears more than a passing resemblance to a very ugly (and miserable) human face.

Fish out of water - in the air this Blobfish is drying out and its skin has begun to rupture (Photo: Claf Hong)

The **American Anglerfish** isn't nicknamed the All-mouth without good reason – it has one of the smallest mouth-to-body ratios of any fish, with its mouth being at least twice as wide as its tail. Living at depths of up to 3,300ft (1,000m), as some Anglerfish do, you need a big mouth to take big bites. Just ask the Umbrella Mouth Gulper Eel (see page 24). Food can often be scarce, and fish that nibble slowly at their dinner risk losing the meal (and maybe their own lives) to scavenging predators that can swallow things whole.

Some types of Anglerfish have a light-up lure to attract their prey (you can read more about fish that go fishing on page 19). Some of the larger types that can grow to 5ft (1.5m) visit the surface if they get hungry, and will grab seabirds that are floating there, taking a breather from flying. Many people probably wouldn't eat an Atlantic Anglerfish if it was served up whole, but a lot of people do in fact eat it and love it, because by the time it is filleted, sliced up and shipped to supermarkets it is called Monkfish or Goosefish instead.

Smile for the camera - no need to ask why the Monkfish is sometimes called the All-mouth (Photo: NOAA)

The **Stomiids** also live in the murky depths, with various members of the family living 250–5,000ft (76.2–1,524m) down. With common names like Dragonfish and Viperfish, what makes the Stomiids so off-putting are their spectacular teeth. Their jaws would surely be enough to make even a shark think twice (though not all sharks are renowned for their intellect). The Dragonfish has a mouthful of fangs that are as sharp as a knife, and if that isn't enough, it also has teeth on its tongue. The Viperfish has barbed bottom teeth so long they can't fit in its mouth, and it needs to use its own backbone as a sort of shock absorber to cushion the impact when it snaps its jaws shut on some unsuspecting prey.

Like the Anglerfish, many Stomiids have a flashing light somewhere on their bodies to lure prey towards them. In fact, quite a lot of deep-sea fish have photophores (organs that light up) for either defensive or offensive purposes (see page 34). Some of these are part of the Dragonfish's diet. The problem with eating bioluminescent fish is that they don't necessarily stop shining after they've been eaten, and if the light is bright enough it can shine through the predator's body. And that makes it highly visible to anything that might want to eat it too. The Dragonfish, however, has a heavily pigmented gut, and the light can't shine through.

Unfortunately, while all of the above look unappetising to our eyes, the problem with trying to look disgusting as a defence mechanism is that many creatures in the oceans don't have eyes that see in the same way as ours do. Some deep-sea fish like the Viperfish have disproportionately large eyes to help them see in the dark, while the freshwater Anableps and the Javelin Spookfish both have four eyes, with the Javelin Spookfish's second pair helpfully growing out of the first pair.

The Javelin Spookfish is related to the **Barreleye**, a fish most famous for having a completely transparent head. Its see-through face serves a similar purpose to the Viperfish's extra large eyes, letting in more light at depths of 1,300–8,200ft (400–2,500m). The Barreleye's eyes look like two passengers sitting on the other side of a windscreen. They are tube-shaped rather than spherical, and can look both up and down at the

Don't trust a Dragonfish - in the dark this Snaggletooth uses that light-up barbel under its chin to lure prey into its mouth (Photo: NOAA)

Flounders are born with one eye on each side – when they grow up one eye actually moves over to the other side (Photo: NOAA)

same time. The Barreleye can be looking upwards for prey, silhouetted against brighter water above, while simultaneously watching out for predators below that are doing the same thing to it.

Four eyes, or two eyes that can look in both directions at once, would certainly help the various types of Flatfish, such as **Flounder**, **Sole** and **Turbot**. They aren't quite so flat when they are born, and have an eye on each side of their head. It's only as they grow up and get flatter that one eye actually migrates to the other side of their body. That's fine if they are lying on the seabed, waiting for prey. But if they are swimming in open water they are completely blind on one side.

Though it doesn't have eyes at all, it would be wrong to call the **Sea Star** blind. More commonly but less accurately referred to as Starfish (it isn't a fish at all), the Sea Star has a mass of light-sensitive cells on the end of each limb. Called ocelli, these cells can detect the presence of light and the direction it is coming from. This is especially helpful if something comes between the Sea Star and a source of light – having a shadow fall over it could let the Sea Star know a predator is nearby.

When crawling along, a Sea Star often holds up one of its limbs to watch out ahead.

Some of the Sea Star's fellow echinoderms, such as the Brittlestar, have ocelli covering the rest of their bodies as well – in effect they see with their skin.

It's hard to sneak up on a Sea Urchin – it might not have a brain, but it can see you coming through its spines (Photo: NOAA)

The **Sea Urchin** doesn't have any eyes either (and they seem to do just fine without a brain too). Instead they see with the spines that cover their body. Light bounces off each spine, so the Sea Urchin can get a sense of something moving around in front of it (or behind it, for that matter). Given that the average Sea Urchin can have several hundred spines, you could say its body is actually one big compound eye.

So most of the creatures in this chapter have specially adapted eyes to help them spot predators. But then nobody (not even most sea life) worries about being attacked by a Sea Star or Turbot! Some predators, however, are also blessed with superior vision, most notably the **Hammerhead Shark**.

Don't blame a Hammerhead if it bites you - its eyes are so far apart it can't see what's in front of its mouth (Photo: Barry Peters)

The distinctive thing about this shark is the way its eyes are set so far apart, at either end of its T-shaped skull. This gives the Hammerhead binocular vision. It can see above, below and behind simultaneously, and has a better sense of distance (how far it is away from rays, squid, people swimming, etc) than most sharks. Of course, this does lead to one significant problem – it has a big blind spot, and can't see what's directly in front of it (or what's going into its mouth). You can read more about the Hammerhead Shark on page 78, and more about its other toothy brothers and sisters in Chapter 6.

Chapter 2
DISGUSTING DIETS

For sharks, everything is on the menu. Things found in their stomachs include car tyres, pieces of wood, unopened and undamaged bottles of wine, and reputedly even a live torpedo. A shark is basically an eating machine – a gut with eyes and a tail. They even have tastebuds in their gullet. While their taste for human flesh is considerably overblown, they do like their meat. The Greenland Shark even hangs around under the ice in the polar waters of the North Atlantic and preys on reindeer and polar bears that fall through the ice.

Most sharks are apex predators. This means that they are at the top of the food chain in their natural environment. Apart from man, sharks have few predators. Of course, the food chain is very long. Pretty much everything that lives in the sea is prey for something else.

Off the Menu!

When we think of seafood we think of something tasty like mussels or scallops. Given the breadth of variety of what's available in the oceans it's quite inexplicable that some creatures in the sea choose truly disgusting things to eat.

The **Snubnosed Eel** is an excellent example. Found in both the Atlantic and Pacific Oceans at depths of 1,600–5,900ft (500–1,800m), the Snubnosed Eel grows to 24in (61cm). When hungry, it attaches itself to its prey, burrows inside and then eats whatever takes its fancy from the swimming buffet. They can live inside their prey for quite some time without killing it. Often they nestle along the prey's backbone, but a Mako Shark was once cut open and two Snubnosed Eels were found living in its heart. In fact, they had been there long enough for the heart tissue to start healing.

The Snubnosed Eel is sometimes called the Slime Eel, but this can be confusing, because Slime Eel is also the nickname of the Hagfish (which has some disgusting eating habits of its own, see page 29).

The **Candiru** drinks blood, hence its common name, the Vampire Catfish. Like other types of catfish (some of which boast tastebuds all over their skin, whilst others can breathe through their skin too) it is actually a freshwater fish, living in the Amazon River. Even though it doesn't technically live in the sea, the Candiru was simply too disgusting to leave out of this book.

The biggest Candiru grow to only 6in (15cm), but the smaller ones are actually the ones you want to avoid the most. Unlike the Snubnosed Eel, the Candiru doesn't gnaw its way into prey. Instead, it takes advantage of orifices that are already available. On a fish this would be its gills, but the Candiru doesn't just attack fish. Once its head is buried deep inside an orifice the Candiru springs a spine so that it can't be removed. Only the tail is left outside, flapping in the water or the air. Even the longest Candiru are only about 0.4in (1cm) wide, which is why the smallest are the worst. Humans have fallen victim to the Candiru, and the lesson learnt from their experience is simple – don't pee in the Amazon River.

Plenty of creatures in the oceans indulge in cannibalism, from the Hammerhead Shark to the Black Swallower (see page 25) as well as various types of lobster, who eat their own newborn babies if the kids don't get away fast enough. Some other sharks don't even last that long. Sand Tiger Sharks are pregnant for two years. During that time her live young eat each other in her womb until there are only a couple left.

But it gets worse. Some types of **Blenny**, most of which live in either tropical or subtropical waters, are what we could politely call coprophages. Or if we weren't being so polite we would say they eat poo. In a way it makes sense. Unless they have a very slow metabolism, most animals excrete digested food that still has nutrients in it. For Blennies these second-hand dinners are simply convenient.

Almost as disgusting as the coprophages are the necrophages. Necrophage fish are carrion feeders, in the same way vultures are on land. Rather than kill their own prey they wait until something else kills it, or it dies of natural causes. The **Osedax**, for example, is a 2in (5cm) worm first discovered off the coast of California in 2002 but later found in the North Sea too. Cheerfully known as the Bone-eating Snot Flower, the Osedax bores into the bones of dead whales to eat the lipids (specifically mineral-rich fats).

Cusk Eels are necrophages, which literally translated from Greek means 'death eater' - they feast on dead things (Photo: NOAA)

Most necrophagic creatures are found at significant depths, such as the **Cusk Eel**, which lives around 6,600ft (2,000m) down. Some members of the Cusk Eel family live even deeper, with one being dredged up from the bottom of the Puerto Rico Trench (almost five and a half miles down), making it the deepest-living sea creature ever discovered. The Cusk Eel needs to live at the bottom of the sea, however deep that is, to eat the carcasses that drift down to the seabed.

The **Grenadier Fish** (also known as the Rattail, because of its thin tapering body) is another necrophage fish. The Giant Grenadier, which grows to 7ft (2.1m), is particularly attracted to shipwrecks in the Pacific Ocean. Despite looking quite demonic, it is harmless to humans – though any drowned sailors who went down with those ships probably ended up as lunch.

Disgusting though necrophages and coprophages are, they actually do a very important ecological job. They keep the oceans clean. Without them it would quickly become choked with excrement and rotting fish flesh. Lots of sea creatures eat things we might find inexplicable, but

Necrophage fish like this Grenadier Fish are important - they help keep the oceans clean of dead matter (Photo: NOAA)

which have a key role in creating a world (both underwater and above it) that we take for granted.

After all, if the **Bumphead Parrotfish** didn't eat coral then it wouldn't excrete fine sand, and without that sand there would be none of those idyllic little islands in the Indian Ocean with their beautiful coral beaches.

How to make a beautiful beach in the Indian Ocean - feed this Bumphead Parrotfish some coral (Photo: NOAA)

Terrible Table Manners

Sea Stars look so cute and innocent it's sometimes difficult to remember that while pretty much everything in the sea is prey for something further up the food chain, pretty much everything in the sea is also a predator for something further down too. For clams, mussels, oysters, and other shellfish, one of those predators is the Sea Star.

When a shellfish realises a hungry Sea Star is coming it will clamp the two halves of its shell tightly shut. Inside its shell, after all, an oyster or a clam is just a soft, fleshy and defenceless blob. The Sea Star has hundreds of sucker-like tube feet on each ray (as its arms are properly

This Sea Star can't be feeding at the moment - its stomach is still inside its body (Photo: NOAA)

known). It uses these to grab hold of its prey, curling its rays around the shell and trying to pull both halves apart. Meanwhile the Sea Star's victim cowers inside, knowing its life depends on the Sea Star not getting the shell open. Unfortunately some Sea Stars can exert a force of up to 30 Newtons with its rays, which is like hanging a 7lb (3.2kg) weight off each shell half. The Sea Star needs only to maintain that grip until its prey gets worn out.

But this is where things get disgusting, because the Sea Star doesn't actually need to open the shell fully before it can feast. As soon as there's a wide enough gap the Sea Star can poke its stomach out of its mouth and slip it into the shell. Inside, the oyster or clam is helpless. The Sea Star's inverted stomach envelops the doomed blob, and then starts releasing strong digestive enzymes. Its prey is still alive when it begins to dissolve. Once the oyster or clam is completely liquidised, the Sea Star sucks its stomach out of the shell and back into its mouth. It actually has a second stomach too, which extracts the nutrients from the juices.

Often the Sea Star leaves nothing behind from its meal but an empty shell. Though they can eat prey bigger than themselves in this way, even the largest Sea Star is only 20in (50cm) between the furthest ray tips. And they can only wrap their stomach around something that's slower than they are, too. Just to be on the safe side, don't stand around barefoot in any tide pools.

Fish Fishing

The **Anglerfish** family includes dozens of slightly different species, but which are all related because of how they catch their prey. Like a guy sitting on a boat, they expect their dinner to be foolish enough to come to them. Given how the first Anglerfish was swimming in the sea over 100 million years ago, they are obviously right not to credit their prey with too much intelligence.

Anglerfish have a sort of fishing pole (called an illicium) that sticks out of the top of their head. At the end of this fishing pole is a glowing lure (called an esca) that the Anglerfish can flash at will. Other fish think the esca is a little bioluminescent creature swimming around. Some Anglerfish wiggle their esca right in front of their jaws. The Barbelled Dragonfish, on the other hand, has an esca on the end of a 6.5ft (2m) barbel – even though its body may only be 6in (15cm) long.

When the curious prey gets close enough to what it thinks is a potential meal, the Anglerfish bolts forward. Its jaws work on an automatic reflex, snapping shut in a fraction of a second. The victim never realises its fatal mistake. Most types of Anglerfish have big enough mouths (and big enough bellies) to eat their prey whole, and one type, Thaumatichthys, actually has the esca inside its mouth.

Other sea creatures go fishing with a sort of net rather than a fishing line. The **Bigfin Squid** lives 6,600ft (2,012m) below and is very rarely seen. It has long, thin tentacles that may be over 20ft (6m) long. Some marine biologists have theorised that the Bigfin Squid drags its tentacles along the seafloor like a bottom-trawling fishing boat, picking up food as it swims. Other marine biologists think it might be more passive than that, and simply wait for fish to bump into its tentacles.

Chaetopterus Pugaporcinus is an underwater annelid, a type of worm similar to an earthworm or a leech. Its Latin name roughly translates to 'resembling a pig's rear', which is why its common name is actually Pigbutt Worm. Looks and name aside, Pugaporcinus also goes fishing with a net. It dangles strings of sticky mucus out of its body

Don't feel sorry for the Anglerfish's prey - they only get eaten because they try to capture that thing above its mouth (Photo: NOAA)

which it uses to capture tiny particles of edible matter floating in the water, such as plankton and bits of dead animals. When it has enough, it sucks the mucus back up.

Some sea creatures that go fishing don't wait around for prey to come to them. The much-feared (and rightly so) **Cone Snail** of the Red Sea makes its land-based cousins look like cuddly pets. Not only can it grow to about 9in (23cm) long, it also has venom many, many times more poisonous than cyanide (you can read more about the most venomous creatures in the sea from page 36).

The Cone Snail eats small fish, molluscs and even other Cone Snails, which it spears with a harpoon-like attachment called a toxoglossan radula. The venom paralyses the prey instantly, but it may still be alive when the Cone Snail starts reeling its harpoon back in like a fishing line. After it's finished eating, the Cone Snail regurgitates anything it couldn't digest, including its harpoon. It can always grow another one.

Though otherworldly and often beautiful, **Sea Anemones** also make use of a sort of harpoon to snare passing fish and shrimp. The tentacles

This type of Sea Anemone is often called the Fish-Eating Anemone – but it sometimes eats passing shrimp too (Photo: NOAA)

of Sea Anemones are armed with venomous cells called nematocysts. These nematocysts have a very sensitive hair that when triggered fires a neurotoxin into whatever triggered it. Paralysed, the fish or shrimp can't move. The Sea Anemone's tentacles then draws its prey into its mouth (which helpfully also doubles as its excretory organ).

Larvacean Lunchboxes

Larvaceans can't be bothered hunting, fishing or trawling for their food. A small form of zooplankton (see page 94), the Larvacean builds a sort of house around itself using proteins and cellulose (simple sugars) produced from its own body. The walls of this bubble work like filters, allowing water to flow through. The water brings microscopic food particles with it, which the filters prevent from flowing out again. The Larvacean needs only to sit and wait until enough water has passed through for the food to build up, and then it can feast. Some Larvaceans keep their house for only a few hours, while others take it with them like a kind of caravan, or a lunchbox.

A Restaurant, a Carwash or a Spa?

You can read more about the unlikely friendships (or at least temporary alliances) that develop between some sea creatures on page 52, but what marine biologists call 'cleaning stations' are a phenomenon that is not only bizarre but more than just a little bit disgusting too.

Cleaning stations are run by **Labroides**, a family of fish better known as **Cleaner Wrasses** precisely because of what they do there. A cleaning station is a place where other fish congregate to be cleaned by a Cleaner Wrasse. Sometimes working in a team with other Cleaner Wrasses (if the client is a big fish), or even joining up with a shrimp who does the same job (perhaps unsurprisingly known as the Cleaner Shrimp), the Cleaners swim all over their client, eating parasites that have attached themselves to the client's scales or skin, as well as dead tissue. It works out well both for Cleaner and client. The client gets all those nasty bugs removed, and the Cleaner gets a ready supply of food delivered to his door like a pizza.

Cleaner Shrimp like this one have to be either very trusting or very stupid to clean the inside of a Moray Eel's mouth – Morays eat shrimp (Photo: NOAA)

Cleaner Wrasses have to be very trusting, because some of the fish that visit cleaning stations (such as Groupers and Snappers) are normally predators that prey on little fish like them. To show they are no threat, and just want cleaning rather than feeding, clients swim in an odd direction or pose in an unusual way. The Parrotfish, for example, rolls over and opens its gills. If clients are really lucky (or find a Cleaner who is very trusting indeed) they can even get cleaned on the inside too. Cleaner Shrimps will swim into the open mouth of a Moray Eel. Some Cleaner Wrasses will enter a client's gills.

Unfortunately, while the clients won't attack the staff of a cleaning station, that doesn't stop them preying on other clients visiting. Fortunately, for those too timid to risk a visit, some Cleaner Wrasses will also make 'house calls', and clean those fish in their own nests and burrows.

The **Combtooth Blenny** is also known as the False Cleanerfish. That's because it lurks around cleaning stations, imitating the colours and behaviour of Cleaner Wrasses. It manages to fool some clients into letting it get close enough to clean them, but instead of eating parasites, the Combtooth Blenny takes a quick nip of skin or scale and then swims away before the client realises it's been tricked.

Cleaner Wrasses shouldn't be confused with Garra Rufa and Cyprinion Macrostomus, the so-called 'doctor fish'. These are the ones originally bred in Turkish spas that eat dead skin. It's an alternative health craze that's spreading through Europe and the US, sitting with your feet in a pool full of hundreds of doctor fish while they nibble away all the dead skin between your toes. Delicious.

Big Teeth and Bigger Bellies

Sharks have several rows of teeth. Unlike human milk teeth, which only get replaced once, shark teeth fall out (or get broken) frequently, and are constantly replaced. A typical carnivorous shark can go through thousands in a lifetime, and each new tooth is a little larger than the one it replaced. So their teeth just keep getting bigger and bigger. Some deep-sea sharks have even been found with their own teeth in their bellies. It's thought they might swallow them to recycle minerals like calcium which are often scarce in the deepest parts of the oceans.

You can read more about the (man-)eating habits of sharks in Chapter 6, but other sea creatures that have mouths to avoid include the **Moray Eel**. The longest type of Moray Eel can grow to 13ft (4m), and because one set of jaws isn't enough, it has a second set in its throat,

No wonder the Fangtooth looks so angry - a hundred thousand years of biting its tongue with teeth like these (Photo: Claf Hong)

called the pharyngeal jaws. The pharyngeal jaws also have teeth, and when the Moray Eel is eating it launches them forward into its mouth, where they clamp down on the ill-fated fish and drag it down into its throat. Fortunately for us, Moray Eels are rather shy and will only attack if their burrows are disturbed. Divers have lost fingers, however, when trying to hand-feed them.

The name **Fangtooth** tells you everything you need to know about this deep-sea fish. Proportionate to their body size, they have the largest teeth of anything in the oceans. In fact, the Fangtooth's fangs are so large they barely fit inside its mouth, and so it has sheath-like sockets on either side of its brain to hold them, like scabbards for swords. The Fangtooth eats other fish in one mouthful, using its giant teeth more for trapping prey in its mouth rather than chewing.

The **Umbrella Mouth Gulper Eel** can also eats its prey whole. It isn't actually an eel, though it has a long tapering body, up to 3.3ft (1m), that resembles an eel's in every way except for its mouth. It's basically just a huge mouth with a tail whipping behind it (and sometimes getting

What a mouth - the Umbrella Mouth Gulper Eel can open its mouth wide enough to eat fish bigger than itself (Photo: Claf Hong)

tied in knots). Often called the Pelican Eel, its jaw is loosely hinged so that it can open its mouth wider than its head. It doesn't need to swim much, it can just drift along, open-mouthed, catching whatever is in its way. Its stomach is elastic, so it can eat large fish, which it deposits in a pouch under its lower jaw, like its namesake.

The **Black Swallower** can also eat fish much larger than itself. Though only 10in (25cm), it has a stomach that can stretch to fit prey twice as long and ten times its own mass. A 19th-century ichthyologist speculated that the Black Swallower grabs a fish by the tail then 'walks' its teeth up the fish's body until it is completely consumed, interlocking its teeth afterwards like bars on a prison.

The Black Swallower usually lives at depths of 2,300–9,000ft (700–2,745m), but some have been caught nearer the surface. They had swallowed fish so big that even their enlarged stomachs couldn't digest the meal before the dead fish started to decompose, and the decomposition gases made the Black Swallower float to the surface.

Chapter 3
DISGUSTING DEFENCES

So if you're a little fish and you don't want to get eaten you're going to have to find a way to defend yourself. Many sea creatures have discovered ingenious ways of doing so, from pretending to be something far more dangerous than themselves, to actually using other animals as weapons. Meanwhile, other species have had to rely on some truly repellent methods of self-defence.

Offensive Defensive

A number of different creatures have an ability to puff themselves up, such as the **Swellshark**, which is normally about 39in (100cm) but can drink enough water to expand to double the size. This way it can lodge itself in crevices which predators (other sharks!) can't remove it from. The **Googly-eyed Glass Squid** (which probably prefers its Latin name, Teuthowenia pellucida) also sucks in a lot of water to puff itself up, appear more threatening and scare predators away. Meanwhile the **Coffinfish**, a type of Anglerfish also known as the Sea Toad, inflates itself with water to make it harder for predators to get a grip – predators can't open their mouths wide enough to bite a puffed-up Coffinfish.

Probably the most famous fish with this ability are the **Porcupinefish** and the **Pufferfish**, which are often mistaken for one another, but have some important differences. Both are slow swimmers, so frequently need to defend themselves from bigger, faster foes. Both can swallow water (its own volume in, as far as the Pufferfish is concerned) to puff themselves up into what looks like a big spiky ball. Both can also swallow air for the same purpose if they have been taken out of the water, by a fisherman or a bird, for example. And both are also venomous, but the Pufferfish's venom is worse (see page 36). Its spines are hidden until it inflates, while the Porcupinefish's spines always stick up. They're also thicker and heavier, like a porcupine's. And the Pufferfish is usually only found in the tropics, but the Porcupinefish can be found in shallow temperate and tropical waters worldwide.

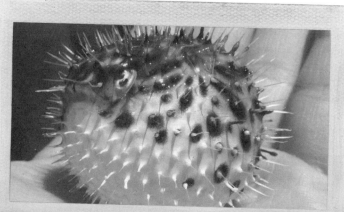

Full of hot air - the Pufferfish can swallow air or water to puff itself up, making its venomous spines stick out (Photo: NOAA)

Like fish that can puff themselves up, the Blanket Octopus can also make itself look bigger in an attempt to scare off predators. Females have a web-like membrane between their legs which when spread out look like a big sheet. Given that females of the species can be 6.6ft (2m) across, that's quite a blanket. Males, on the other hand, don't have this ability, but then they only grow to the size of a walnut. Female Blanket Octopuses also have another means to defend themselves. They are immune to the venom of the Portuguese Man of War (see page 93), so they can rip off its tentacles and use them as weapons against predators who aren't immune. Handy!

All **Octopuses** are venomous, but only a few (such as the Blue-Ringed Octopus, see page 36) are particularly harmful to humans. Aside from camouflage, most species rely on their ability to squirt a thick cloud of dark ink for defence. As the cloud spreads rapidly in the water the Octopus can flee, and the attacking predator won't see which way it went. Some predators will attack the ink, perhaps hoping the Octopus is simply hiding. Of course, in the dark depths of the oceans, where predators don't just rely on sight, a cloud of ink isn't quite as useful. However, it's thought the ink also has a potent smell that can distract predators with strong noses, like sharks.

While most people know pearls come from the shells of molluscs like **oysters**, they don't know that the oyster constructs the pearl as a defence mechanism. A pearl is just a by-product of an immune system type response. If a parasite (or even just a grain of sand) gets into its shell when it opens up to feed, the oyster builds a sac around it, then starts laying down layers of calcium carbonate deposits to seal the intruder in, trap it and (if it's alive) kill it. Pearl farmers artificially stimulate the production of a pearl by inserting something into the oyster's shell.

Octopuses can defend themselves so well you'd think predators would give up and eat something else – this one certainly hopes so (Photo: NOAA)

CREATURE FEATURE
Hagfish a.k.a. Slime Eel

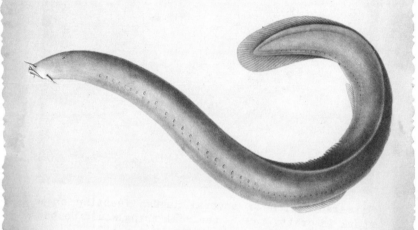

Fishermen, marine biologists and pretty much everyone else who has ever encountered one all seem to agree – out of 230,000 known species, the Hagfish is by far the most disgusting creature that inhabits the oceans.

The Hagfish is actually neither a fish nor an eel. An invertebrate, with a skull but no spine, the Hagfish is like a long sea worm. Often pinkish grey in colour, and slightly flattened, the Hagfish looks a bit like a tongue – a tongue that can grow to be 50in (127cm) long.

The Hagfish got its Slime Eel nickname for a good reason. Glands covering its body secrete mucus, literally by the bucketful. The mucus reacts with water to turn into a sticky goo which then expands. A fully grown Hagfish can exude enough mucus to turn a bucket of water into jelly in only a few minutes. The mucus is not Hagfish snot. It contains fibres which bond together, making the jelly strong and hard to remove.

The mucus is a fantastic defence mechanism. It makes the Hagfish slippery, which means it's hard for predators to keep a hold, and if a fish tries to bite a Hagfish the mucus can get into the fish's gills and suffocate it.

This recreation of several Hagfish feasting on a shark is pretty tame - the real thing would be too disgusting to print (Photo: Ryan Somma)

However, the Hagfish also has another party piece. When threatened it will turn its head round and tie itself in an overhand knot. It then moves this knot down its body, squeezing out even more mucus. If you grabbed hold of a Hagfish it would force this knot toward your hand and, its body being so slimy, the knot would force you to lose your grip.

But it gets worse. The Hagfish can either be a scavenger of a parasite, depending on what comes floating by the sand or silt on the seabed where it spends much of its time. While its core diet consists of marine worms, the Hagfish will also prey on larger animals. It will often eat them from the inside, which is the safest place to be if your prey is bigger than you. The Hagfish enters through the gills (or other orifices), eats the intestines first and then proceeds to tuck into anything else that takes its fancy. Cod have been caught with several dozen Hagfish attached to them.

A nest of Hagfish - apparently they taste great chopped up and stir-fried with chilli paste and garlic (Photo: NOAA)

Scientists are currently investigating possible uses for Hagfish slime, such as an emergency treatment for flesh wounds, because it is both stretchy and strong. Hagfish meat is also considered something of a treat in Japan and Korea, where five million pounds of it are eaten every year. Apparently it tastes great in a stir fry with chilli paste and garlic. Hagfish mucus can also be used as a substitute for egg whites, because it has a similar chemical make-up and the same texture.

Suddenly jellied eels don't sound so bad, do they?

Masters of Disguise

Some sea creatures were lucky enough to be born with a natural form of camouflage, such as the **Comet Fish**, a favourite snack of the Moray Eel. It's no coincidence that the Comet Fish's tail looks exactly like a Moray Eel's tail. Should a Moray Eel come along, all the Comet Fish needs to do is stick its head in a crevice and with any luck the Moray Eel will swim past thinking it just saw one of its pals.

Unfortunately this might not prove such a great disguise if a Barracuda swims past instead. They prey on Moray Eels. Likewise if something that eats seaweed spots a **Leafy Sea Dragon**, its camouflage could lead to disaster. The Leafy Sea Dragon, which is related to the Seahorse, looks like a few loose fronds of seaweed. It drifts slowly through the waters off Australia as if it really is just a plant carried by the currents.

The **Carpet Shark** (known in Australia by its Aboriginal name, Wobbegong) looks like a big seafloor-coloured rug, complete with a fringe (which looks like weeds). It spends much of its time on the

If you were a Comet Fish you'd want to hide from this Moray Eel too - Morays have a second pair of jaws waiting in their throat (Photo: NOAA)

seabed, where its colours and markings help it blend in. So good is its camouflage, in fact, that the normally docile Carpet Shark has given nasty bites to divers who accidentally step on one.

The best way to scare off predators – disguise yourself as a bunch of Sea Snakes like this Mimic Octopus is doing (Photo: Steve Childs)

However, the undisputed master of disguise must surely be the **Mimic Octopus** of southeast Asia. Many types of Octopus can change their colours to blend in with their environment. The Mimic Octopus is the only one that actually imitates other sea creatures. Growing to 2ft (60cm), the Mimic Octopus can change its colour and its markings, adopting vivid stripes along its arms so that they look like sea snakes. Sea snakes are a predator of many species, who now see eight of them.

But the Mimic Octopus goes even further, contorting its body, folding in its arms and adopting the movements of other creatures. It can make its arms look like the wings of a Stingray, and will use them to swim like one too. Stingray prey keep their distance, even if they would happily eat a Mimic Octopus. The Mimic Octopus also uses this trick to catch its own dinner, pretending to be a crab, walking across the seafloor like one, until it gets close enough to another one to eat it.

The slug-like **Sea Hare** shares a few tactics with octopuses, such as squirting ink to act as a distraction while it evades predators. The ink can be poisonous to some fish. The Sea Hare can also change its colour depending on what it eats. This is a very clever trick when you think about it – it means the Sea Hare blends in against its food and is perfectly camouflaged when eating.

Of course the best form of camouflage for any animal would be invisibility. Numerous sea creatures almost manage this by having transparent bodies, such as the **Humpback Anglerfish**, which lives in the dark depths where what little light there is just passes straight through it, and the **Cystisoma**, which looks like a shrimp made of glass. The **Glass Squid** isn't quite so transparent – its digestive organ is still visible, and might prove a tempting target for a hungry predator.

The four-eyed **Javelin Spookfish** manages the next best thing to transparency, which is to be translucent. The shallower water overhead is always lighter, so from the perspective of predators below, everything has a silhouette. At least by being translucent the Javelin Spookfish lets some of the light through.

Let There Be Light!

The **Hatchetfish** is a favourite food of Barreleye fish like the Javelin Spookfish. The Barreleye can look up continuously, watching for prey that is silhouetted against the shallower, lighter waters overhead. The Hatchetfish has a clever trick called counter illumination. It has photophores (light-producing organs) along its side that match the intensity of the light above exactly. The Barreleye thinks it sees only brighter water above it, even when it's looking straight at the faintly glowing shape of a Hatchetfish.

Unfortunately while several creatures use photophores for defence in this way, there are plenty of predators that use light to help them catch their prey. The Anglerfish's antics are described on page 19. The **Cookiecutter Shark**, on the other hand, gives off a green glow from its entire body – except for a dark patch near its head. To another fish swimming nearby, that dark patch might look like a small creature swimming between it and the Cookiecutter. The Cookiecutter wants the curious fish to think the creature might be easy prey, because then it can pounce.

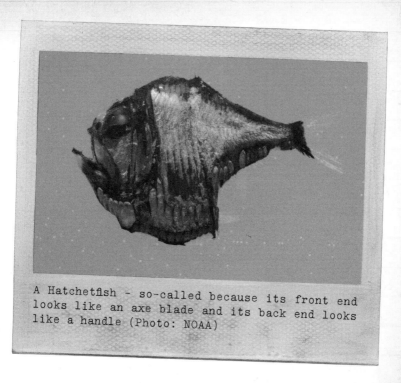

A Hatchetfish - so-called because its front end looks like an axe blade and its back end looks like a handle (Photo: NOAA)

Some types of **Cuttlefish** also use light as a weapon. They can flash bright colours like yellow, red and turquoise in a beautiful display that has a hypnotic effect on the Cuttlefish's victim. As if stunned, it doesn't move as the Cuttlefish's tentacles shoot out from inside its beak to drag the prey back into its mouth. Similarly, the **Dana Octopus Squid** (it's definitely a squid) uses blinding flashes of light from photophores on its arms to disorientate potential prey before sweeping in to attack.

In Japan, the **Ostracod** (a shrimp-like form of plankton) is also known as the Sea Firefly. They can be seen glowing blue in shallow Pacific waters. Their glow survives after they die. During the Second World War, Japanese soldiers would catch them in traps, dry them out and ground them into a powder, which they took with them. Adding a little water to the Ostracod powder would make it glow again, producing just enough light for the soldiers to read maps and things without needing to use a torch or a flame that might give away their position.

Beautiful but deadly - Pfeffer's Flamboyant Cuttlefish has venom many times more powerful than cyanide (Photo: Silke Baron)

Toxic Top Ten

Some of the most venomous creatures in the sea are also the most venomous in the entire animal kingdom. Poison is a highly effective means of self-defence, especially when only small amounts are needed to kill a predator. Even a tiny fish becomes fearsome if it has enough venom to kill dozens of adult humans.

The most prevalent poison amongst venomous creatures is tetrodotoxin, which can be found in the **Pufferfish** (the second-most poisonous vertebrate in the world after the Golden Poison Frog) and **Porcupinefish**, the giant **Ocean Sunfish**, and some species of **Cone Snail**, which have reportedly killed people who accidentally stepped on them. It is also found in the beautiful but deadly Pfeffer's **Flamboyant Cuttlefish** and the **Blue-Ringed Octopus**, two of the world's most poisonous animals.

Tetrodotoxin has no antidote. Even the smallest Blue-Ringed Octopus, only the size of a golf ball, carries enough of it to kill 30 adult men. Just 0.00002oz (or half a mg, in other words) is enough to kill

Warning signs - if the blue rings of the Blue-Ringed Octopus start to pulsate that means it's getting agitated (Photo: Angell Williams)

you. Cyanide would need a lot more. However, tetrodotoxin isn't always lethal. The neurotoxin causes paralysis, particularly of the diaphragm, which is necessary for breathing. Sufficient doses also paralyse the heart, causing cardiac arrest. Someone who has been poisoned will need artificial respiration and CPR for several hours as they won't be able to breathe for themselves, nor will their heart be able to pump blood. The good news is that if you are poisoned with tetrodotoxin but survive the first 24 hours you will probably make a full recovery.

Don't go swimming in the Red Sea without health insurance. A disproportionate number of venomous creatures can be found swimming in its warm waters, from the Pufferfish to the Triggerfish (another one armed with tetrodotoxin) to the **Reef Stonefish**, the world's most deadly fish.

Growing to about 20in (51cm), the Reef Stonefish can be found all over the Pacific and Indian Oceans and, in case being ugly and poisonous wasn't bad enough, can even survive out of water for almost a day. It proves a real hazard to divers, as its venom can kill in hours, causing pain so excruciating that people have screamed that they want their stung limb amputated. Fortunately, this time, there is an antidote.

Apparently the stings of the **Lionfish** and **Scorpionfish** are almost as painful as the Reef Stonefish's. They can also cause vomiting, fever, sometimes kill too, and yes, they make their home in the Red Sea as well.

Going on the numbers alone, the deadliest animal in the world is the **Box Jellyfish**, which isn't actually a jellyfish at all. In the last 130 years a reported 5,500 people have been killed by the creature. Also known as the Sea Wasp, one Box Jellyfish can kill dozens of people, and in Australia the authorities put nets around beaches to stop them reaching swimmers. Helpfully the Box Jellyfish is transparent, so difficult to see in the water. However, a Box Jellyfish sting is not always lethal. There is an antidote, but by way of first aid, vinegar should be applied to the sting. The acid prevents any more of the poisonous nematocysts embedded in the skin from injecting more venom. It is a complete myth that urine can be used to treat such stings.

It's not all bad - some people with arthritis have reported less pain and better mobility after being stung by a Reef Stonefish (Photo: NOAA)

The Box Jellyfish is a cnidarian, a cousin to so-called 'true' jellyfish, like the notorious **Irukandji** of northern Australia. Even the name makes this one sound monstrous. It has its own syndrome, Irukandji Syndrome, to describe the symptoms caused by its venom: cramps, vomiting, excruciating pain, cardiac arrest, death. Don't let the Irukandji's size fool you. It may only be the size of a fingernail, but its tentacles can reach 3.3ft (1m), and they contain venom 100 times more powerful than a cobra's. Supposedly some Irukandji were found living in the water supply in Derby – that might be an urban legend, but it might not be.

Many **sea snakes** are actually more poisonous than their land-based cousins. The only reason they don't prove as lethal is because they inject less venom when they bite. Sea snakes come into contact

In 1932 millions of Sea Snakes were seem swarming off the coast of Malaysia - the swarm was 62 miles (100km) long (Photo: NOAA)

with swimmers in the Indian and Pacific Oceans because they can't breathe underwater. They need to surface regularly to take a breath. Sea snakes grow to 3.9–4.9ft (1.2–1.5m) and the largest are still capable of killing an adult human. Their venom initially causes flu-like symptoms, followed by muscle breakdown, renal failure (where the kidneys can no longer detoxify the blood), then cardiac arrest.

Seaweed of Death from Hana is a good name for an anemone-like coral found near Hawaii that contains the poison palytoxin. Palytoxin, which can also be found in the Palythoa Coral, can kill a few hundred healthy adults with only a few drops. Even lesser doses cause loss of breath, chest pains and a racing pulse.

Despite its reputation, one species that shouldn't really be on this list is the **Stingray**, a much misunderstood creature that only uses its barbed tail in self-defence, and only as a last resort if it can't just swim away. After wildlife expert and TV personality Steve Irwin was killed by one in 2006 some people in Australia caught Stingrays in revenge

Watch where you step – Stingrays often hide in the sand and most people who get stung accidentally wade over one (Photo: NOAA)

attacks and left their mutilated, tail-less bodies to rot on Queensland beaches.

But as a fellow expert pointed out after watching footage of the 'attack', the Stingray only swiped Irwin after he accidentally cornered it. And he wasn't killed by its venom, which is rarely lethal to humans, but because the Stingray impaled him through the chest, damaging vital blood vessels.

Another creature that probably shouldn't be on this list either (because it isn't venomous at all) is the **Glaucus**. Some other sea slugs have toxins that cause a racing heartbeat and low blood pressure in predators, but the Glaucus deserves a mention here for what it does with Portuguese Man of War venom. It is immune to the venom itself, and when it eats the Man of War's tentacles its gut absorbs the poison rather than digesting it, and then passes the toxins out through its skin. So the Glaucus doesn't need to be toxic to defend itself. It uses its prey's venom to do that.

That's more than ten sea creatures in the Toxic Top Ten. As you can probably appreciate, there are so many venomous creatures in the oceans it would be hard to narrow them down.

Offensive Offensive

Offence is often the best form of defence, as the saying goes. Many creatures have defensive abilities they use for hunting too, such as the **Electric Eel** (which isn't actually an eel but a freshwater knifefish, similar to a catfish). Growing to 6ft (1.8m), the Electric Eel not only uses electricity for self-defence and hunting, it also uses it for communication and navigation too. It can produce up to 500 volts from 5,000–6,000 stacked electroplaques, which work like the chemical cells in a battery. These electricity-producing organs make up much of its body. A charge of that level could kill a man. By comparison, the Electric Ray can only produce about 200 volts, but that's still equivalent to dropping an electrical appliance into a bath.

The **American Lobster** (or, as it's more specifically known within the US, the Maine Lobster) has not one but two bladders, and they are located within its head. Like a dog, the American Lobster uses urine to mark out its territory with its own scent. However, unlike a dog, the American Lobster can also use these nozzles as a sort of weapon, squirting plumes of urine up to 5ft (1.5m), more than three times its own body length. It can increase the range by building up water pressure

Forget the claws - the nastiest thing this American Lobster can do is shoot you with urine from the twin bladders in its head (Photo: NOAA)

with its gills and mouth. It mainly uses this against rival lobsters, but, being a romantic crustacean, it also uses its double-barrelled pee gun to attract a mate.

As you'd expect from something nicknamed the Pistol Shrimp, the **Crinoid Snapping Shrimp** also has a sort of gun. Even though it only shoots air, a 2in (5cm) Crinoid Snapping Shrimp can create a wave of bubbles strong enough to break glass. So you can imagine the effect it has on predator or prey. It creates these cavitation bubbles (as they are properly known) with its enlarged claw, which may be more than half its total body length. The other claw isn't quite so big, but on the big one the Crinoid Snapping Shrimp has a hammer-like feature that can snap down, much like the hammer in a real gun. The air in the bubbles travels at 60mph. It sounds like a gun going off too.

You wouldn't want to keep a **Mantis Shrimp** in an aquarium, primarily because it would smash its way out in no time. The Mantis Shrimp can also create cavitation bubbles with its claw, though instead of having a gun-like firing mechanism it can simply swipe that claw at

Your thumbs are safe for now - this Mantis Shrimp's powerful claws are folded up behind its head (Photo: NOAA)

incredible speed – almost as fast as a bullet. The Mantis Shrimp isn't actually a shrimp at all. Growing to lengths of up to 15in (38cm), it has arguably the most powerful claws in nature. They have earned the Mantis Shrimp the nickname 'thumbsplitter'. Its cavitation bubbles hit prey with a force of 1,500 Newtons, so it's like being hit by a truck. Oysters and other molluscs stand no chance.

The **Shortfin Mako Shark** can create cavitation bubbles too, swiping its tail swiftly in the water to help it prey on dolphins and even other sharks. You can read more about the offensive habits of sharks in Chapter 6, but another shark's tail to avoid would be that of the Thresher Shark. About 16ft (5m) in length, with the upper lobe of its tail as long as the rest of its body, the **Thresher Shark** can use its tail like a whip, knocking out prey and sometimes inflicting nasty injuries even before it gets its teeth into them. It was never proven whether a Thresher Shark really cut a fisherman's head off with its tail once, but those who hunt the species for sport like to believe it's true.

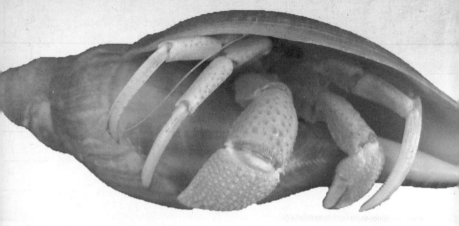

Chapter 4
DISGUSTING HABITS

Even if you ignore how they eat or defend themselves, some sea creatures have truly disgusting personal habits. But if you haven't been put off ever swimming in the sea again by creatures that can bite you, poison you, electrocute you, slime you, decapitate you, suck your blood, burrow inside your body or shoot you in the face with their pee, then you shouldn't have any problem with creatures that like to lay their eggs inside a living host.

The Most Hated Creatures in the Sea

Despite its name, the **Tongue-Eating Louse** doesn't actually eat tongues. Though small at 1.5in (3.8cm), when you consider that it looks like a woodlouse, that would make it the biggest woodlouse you have ever seen. The Red Snapper hates the Tongue-Eating Louse, and with good reason. The Tongue-Eating Louse enters the fish through its gills and swims up into its mouth. There it stabs its claws into the muscles at the base of the Snapper's tongue and proceeds to suck the blood out of it until the tongue dies and drops off.

But that's only the beginning of the Tongue-Eating Louse's relationship with the Red Snapper. With the tongue gone the Tongue-Eating Louse makes itself comfortable in the Red Snapper's mouth, sitting in the place of its tongue, happily drinking bodily fluids and sucking blood direct from an artery. The Red Snapper can live quite a while with a Tongue-Eating Louse squatting inside its head.

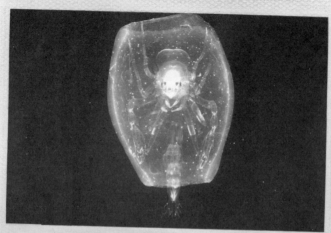

Like something out of a horror movie, the female Phronima eats her way inside a Salp and then lays her larvae (Photo: Getty)

The barrel-shaped jelly-bodied Salp has an equally good reason to hate the **Phronima**, a transparent shrimp-like amphipod found in every ocean of the world (except at the poles). A female Phronima will latch onto a Salp and use her mouth and claws to burrow into it. She then proceeds to eat the poor Salp from the inside. But this isn't just about getting a good meal. Once she has hollowed out her Salp, the female Phronima lays her eggs inside. Then she rides around, using the hollow Salp corpse as a sort of submarine where her larvae can develop in safety. The Phronima's natural enemies don't realise so don't attack. Of course, the Salp's natural enemies don't know any better either.

Red Snappers hate Tongue-Eating Lice. Salps hate Phronimas. Everyone hates the infamously nefarious **Lamprey**. For 400 million years this eel-like jawless fish has plagued temperate waters with its round sucker mouth full of rows and rows of tiny sharp teeth. After attaching itself to its victim (commonly medium-sized fish), the Lamprey uses its tongue (which also has little teeth on) to chew a hole. Its saliva has anticoagulant properties, which means it stops the fish's blood clotting. The Lamprey then sucks the victim's body juices out through its funnel-like mouth.

Not all Lampreys suck blood - their name comes from a hybrid of Latin and Greek words meaning 'stone licker' (Photo: Enrique Dans)

Just like with the Hagfish, fish can sometimes be caught with several Lamprey hanging off them. They probably wouldn't be very big Lampreys, however. The largest type grows to 40in (100cm), and several of those could drain a fish quickly. Some female Lampreys do have a soft, cuddly side, however. They have been seen stacking stones to build a protective nest for their offspring.

You wouldn't want to be a male **Deep-Sea Anglerfish**. While the female of the species is about 5in (12.7cm) long, the male only grows to the size of a small human finger. It has a short and unpleasant life, its sole ambition to find a female to latch onto. Indeed, if it doesn't attach to a female with its small hooked teeth, it will starve to death.

Once it has bitten a female, the male Deep-Sea Anglerfish can never let go. The first thing that happens is that enzymes in the female's body actually dissolve both her flesh and his mouth so that they become fused together. He spends the rest of his life as a parasite. One by one his organs shut down because he no longer needs them. His digestive organs go first because he gets his food from her. Their blood vessels are also connected, so he no longer needs a heart either. He doesn't need to see, so he loses his eyes. And he doesn't need to think, so he loses his brain too.

From the female's perspective, when she needs a mate, she has one ready. In fact, she might be spoilt for choice, because some female Deep-Sea Anglerfish have been caught with several brainless males hanging off them.

You don't need to read Chapter 6 to know you probably shouldn't pick on sharks. That makes some **Copepods** either ultra brave or ultra foolish. Looking like tiny transparent woodlice, some have adhesion pads to attach themselves to shark fins, while others have claws to dig into the shark's skin. They feed on secretions and blood, and can annoy their host shark so much that even the rather laidback Basking Shark is thought to jump out of the water to try to shake them off. Given that sharks have been seen with Copepods attached to their eyeballs, that's perhaps not surprising.

Remoras are also known as Shark Suckers. Watch footage of the 40ft (12.2m) Whale Shark swimming and you will probably see several of these elongated fish dangling off its side. They also latch onto smaller sharks, as well as whales, large rays, sea turtles and even human divers. The Remora has a ridged sucker on the top of its head. The least parasitic Remoras just snack on skin parasites while its host transports

The top of the Remora's head has vertical slats
- it can also attach to the hulls of boats, and
to scuba divers' skin (Photo: NOAA)

it to a new location. Some Remoras, however, will steal scraps from the shark's meal or even feast on a female shark's placenta if it gives birth.

Deserving a mention here is the **Hermit Crab**. There would be few sea snails in the Hermit Crab fan club. The Hermit Crab, which is found all over the world, is born without a thick exoskeleton (which actually means it's not really a true crab). Its abdomen is soft and fleshy, so it needs to find a shell for protection. Usually this means stealing one from a sea snail. However, these aquatic squatters can use anything (even bits of hollow driftwood or a rock with a hole in it), providing it can carry the weight, and most importantly can't be removed from it.

The ideal shell for a Hermit Crab is one that's quite a snug fit, so that it can hide inside if a predator approaches, and the predator can't pull it out. Of course, Hermit Crabs keep on growing (and some can live for 30 years, if they're lucky), so they need to replace their stolen shells from time to time. Some species have a sort of chain of ownership. When one Hermit Crab finds a larger shell to move into, other Hermit Crabs gather around, and when the largest moves into his new shell, the next largest moves into his old one, and so on, right down to the smallest. Sometimes if more than one Hermit Crab finds a shell that is perfectly sized for both of them they will fight over it.

This Hermit Crab stole the shell of a giant sea snail - other Hermit Crabs settle for hollow stones or pieces of driftwood (Photo: NOAA)

CREATURE FEATURE
The Sea Cucumber

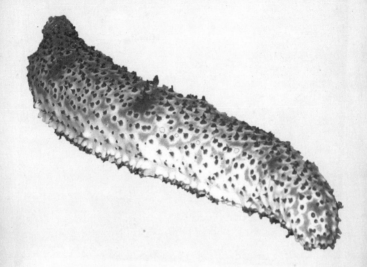

Despite the name, you probably wouldn't want to put any **Sea Cucumber** in your sandwiches (though in some parts of the world they do). Like a big prickly underwater slug with a fanged sucker at one end, the Sea Cucumber is very popular with **Pearl Fish**. But it's probably fair to say the feeling isn't mutual.

If a Pearl Fish is threatened and there's a Sea Cucumber around the Pearl Fish will swim up into the Sea Cucumber's bowels and remain there until the danger has passed. It wriggles in backwards using its long pointy tail to guide it. Of course, when it gets up there it might find the Sea Cucumber's bowels are already a little crowded.

The **Pea Crab** (which, fortunately for the Sea Cucumber, is named for its size) also likes to hide up a Sea Cucumber's backside, as do certain types of polychaete worm. But that's not all. The Sea Cucumber even has its own genus of mollusc, Entovalva, which only live within its digestive system. There's also a type of sea snail called Enteroxenos Ostergreni which, on reaching adulthood, ditches its shell (along with most of its major organs) and spends the rest of its days living like an egg-spreading worm inside a Sea Cucumber.

A mouth at each end - what goes into a Sea Cucumber's digestive tract is only slightly less disgusting than what comes out (Photo: NOAA)

Sea Cucumbers live on the seafloor. Though the largest species can grow to almost 30in (76.2cm) most are around 6–10in (15–25cm). They come in a variety of vivid colours from a vibrant blue to a brilliant red, and may look spiky, frilly or even furry in appearance. The Sea Cucumber has rows of small tube feet which extend and retract using hydraulics to allow it to crawl slowly across the seabed. Some extract food from the water, while others sweep the mud or sand with mucus-laden tentacles. It alternates tentacles, sweeping with one while licking the other. Nerve endings in the skin give the Sea Cucumber sensitivity to light and touch, but it has no true brain.

To make up for that, it has two mouths, though the second one is also its anus. The Sea Cucumber eats with the mouth at one end, and excretes and breathes through the mouth at the other end. When it opens its anal 'mouth', seawater flows in and washes over the Sea Cucumber's respiratory organs. It's at this point that the Pearl Fish might try to sneak in. Some Sea Cucumbers even have teeth around their back passage to try and put them off.

The Sea Cucumber's many uninvited guests find its bowels well stocked with nutritious bacteria. They can also eat nutrients that the Sea Cucumber ate for itself but which have passed through its body undigested. However, if a peckish Pearl Fish decides to nibble on one of the Sea Cucumber's internal organs it might find itself swiftly ejected – along with those internal organs (it can regenerate them in about a month).

This is a defence mechanism the Sea Cucumber also uses against predators, because unlike the Pearl Fish many sea creatures are not immune to the Sea Cucumber's toxic digestive juices. Some Sea Cucumbers can even turn themselves inside out so that their poisonous innards are now outtards, and predators dare not take a bite.

That's not the only clever trick the Sea Cucumber has for defending itself. It can also change its body state. It can go from solid and hard one moment to almost liquid the next. So when in danger it can find a narrow crack, turn its body into mush, slip through the crack, then solidify into hard lumps on the other side. Predators can't extract it. The Sea Cucumber can do this because it has a form of collagen in its skin which can excrete or absorb water, becoming harder the more water it has absorbed.

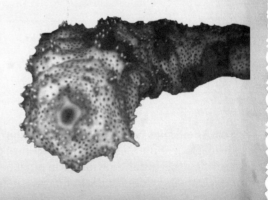

Unlikely Friends

Not all sea creatures who find themselves living together have a parasitic relationship. Some form temporary alliances, usually for defence or hunting purposes, from which both creatures benefit.

The **Portuguese Man of War**, for example, lets various fish who are immune to its venom shelter within its poisonous tentacles, which can grow up to 165ft (50m). Commonly mistaken for a jellyfish, the Man of War is actually a siphonophore – not a single creature but a colony of many smaller ones (see page 93). Many of the smaller fish who are unaffected by the Man of War's venom attract larger ones that are. By protecting the little ones instead of eating them, the Man of War can use them as bait for a bigger dinner.

Best of friends - the Clownfish is immune to Sea Anemone venom, and may act as bait for the Sea Anemone's dinner (Photo: NOAA)

Sea Anemones have a similar relationship with the Clownfish (to the extent where the Clownfish is sometimes called the Anemonefish instead). The beautiful Clownfish can often be found bobbing around in the gently swaying tentacles of various types of Sea Anemone in the Pacific and Indian Oceans. It would be easy to believe the tentacles aren't poisonous at all.

The Sea Anemone protects the Clownfish from predators who either know better than to get too close to those tentacles, or who quickly find out. Some marine biologists have theorised the Clownfish's bright colours also attract other fish for the Sea Anemone to eat. But the main job the Clownfish does in return for protection is to keep the Sea Anemone clean of parasites and small invertebrates. The Sea Anemone often leaves the Clownfish scraps from its meals, but the Sea Anemone sometimes eats the undigested nutrients in the Clownfish's excreta, so the Clownfish probably wouldn't want to eat its own dinner a second time.

Some types of Sea Anemone hitchhike with the Hermit Crab. Sea Anemones can't move far (or fast) on their own, so Hermit Crabs sometimes give them a ride to a new feeding ground. The Sea Anemone clings to the Hermit Crab's stolen shell and uses its tentacles to fend off

Some types of Grouper Fish can grow to over 7ft (2m) - no wonder they need Moray Eels to help flush out prey hiding in small crevices (Photo: NOAA)

any of the Hermit Crab's predators (or perhaps just someone else who wants that shell).

Creatures that team up with other species with different aims are quite common, but creatures that form alliances for the same shared purpose are very rare. In the sea the only two species that cooperate to hunt together are the **Grouper Fish** and the **Giant Moray Eel**.

Groupers are typically large stout fish, wider than they are high, and with big mouths. Prey can escape them by swimming into narrow hiding places where the Grouper's mouth won't fit. Unfortunately for the prey, Giant Moray Eels may grow to 13ft (4m) long, but remain thin. A hungry Grouper initiates an alliance with a Moray by shaking its head. The Moray Eel then swims into cracks and crevices where prey might be hiding. Either the Moray flushes it out, or brings it out dead. Either way, the Grouper and its Moray partner then share the meat between them.

Only predators tend to live a solitary existence. Many sea creatures live with others of their own kind because there truly is safety in numbers. Not many, however, live with creatures from a completely different species, but **Gobies** and some **shrimp** show how it can work. The shrimp digs a burrow for them both while the Goby stands guard. Many shrimp have poor eyesight. Sometimes they don't even see the Goby retreat into the burrow because a predator is nearby, and the Goby has to flick the shrimp with its tail as a warning. The shrimp then follows the Goby inside, and they both wait until the danger has passed.

Without a Goby on the door, a Pistol Shrimp will often hide in its burrow with only its antennae sticking out. If unsuspecting prey passes by the Pistol Shrimp can fire its bubble gun (see page 42) from indoors and only come out to drag its freshly killed dinner back inside.

Our human impulse at the mention of bacteria is to grab the bleach. But for many sea creatures, bacteria is their best friend. The **Pompeii Worm**, for example, relies on a thick coat of bacteria to stop it being cooked alive.

On land, volcanoes sit along the edges of tectonic plates, where the earth's crust is split open and molten magma from deep inside the planet can rise up to the surface (and in the event of an eruption, above it). Of course these tectonic splits in the earth's crust also happen underwater. This leads to hydrothermal vents, which are like hot springs on the seabed. They may be thousands of feet (or even metres) down, where the water is normally around freezing, but near hydrothermal vents the

An unlikely alliance - two Gobies and a Pistol Shrimp stand guard over the burrow they all share (Photo: Andreas März)

water temperature can reach 176°F (80°C). Few creatures can live in that kind of environment.

And if it wasn't for its bacterial mates, the Pompeii Worm couldn't either. Named for the Ancient Roman city destroyed by the eruption of Mount Vesuvius in 79AD, the Pompeii Worm is a 5in (13cm) polychaete worm frequently called a Bristle Worm. That's because it has so much bacteria clinging to its body that it looks furry. The bacteria can be layered almost half an inch (1.3cm) thick. While the bacteria provides a sort of thermal insulation for the Pompeii Worm, the Pompeii Worm keeps the bacteria fed with mucus it secretes from glands on its back.

The **Riftia Tube Worm** also lives near hydrothermal vents in the Pacific, and also relies on bacteria living inside it. In fact, your average Riftia Tube Worm has an entire colony living inside it, in a special and unique organ called a trophosome. Bacteria can account for half the Tube Worm's body weight, and Tube Worms are big – taller than you and as thick as your leg. Tube Worms have no stomach and no

It might look like a plant, but this Tube Worm is actually an invertebrate - an animal without a backbone (Photo: NOAA)

mouth, but they don't need them. The bacteria in their trophosomes consume poisonous chemicals like hydrogen sulphide that spout from the hydrothermal vents and turn them into organic molecules that the Tube Worm finds nutritious, and quite possibly delicious too.

It's Not All Happy Families

Boy meets girl, girl has babies, boy dies, girl becomes a boy, boy has babies, boy eats babies – the cycle of life under the sea is like a crazy soap opera. Freezing waters full of hungry predators make the oceans a pretty inhospitable place to bring up a family, which might explain some of the quirks various sea creatures have developed.

While the male **American Lobster** uses its pee gun for fighting or self-defence (see page 41), the female uses it to attract a mate. She

Only the quickest lobsters survive - their parents eat the slow ones right after they're born (Photo: NOAA)

shoots urine into holes where she thinks there might be a male hiding. Before she can get pregnant a female must shed her shell. Outside of a shell a lobster is just a soft, fleshy gelatinous creature, so the female then has to spend her pregnancy hiding while it regrows. Meanwhile the father of her children sometimes eats her old shell. But that's not the only disgusting thing he eats. Once born, the baby lobsters had better get out of there quick. Only the quickest newborn lobsters survive, because the parents eat the slow ones.

You wouldn't want to kiss a lobster, even if you were another lobster. Living on the mouthparts of some lobsters are **Symbion Pandora**, little insect-like creatures who help themselves to bits of the lobster's lunch. The female Symbion Pandora can turn herself into an egg. She sticks to the lobster's shell like a hard lump and eventually larvae will hatch out of her. They then swim off to find lobster lips of their own, where they feed until it's their turn to reproduce.

The Symbion Pandora isn't the only sea creature to use other living things as a nest for their offspring. For example, one type of Snailfish (which looks like a giant pink tadpole) lays its eggs in the gills of King Crabs. And barnacles don't just stick to wooden docks and the hulls of boats. One type, **Sacculina**, attaches itself to female crabs. It crawls over the crab's shell until it finds a crack on the underside of her thorax to inject itself into. Then it grows an egg sac out of the crab, which replaces the crab's own. The crab won't be able to have children any more, but instead cares for the Sacculina's eggs as her own. She will even stir the water to help the newborn Sacculina swim away.

In most of nature we are used to hearing about the alpha male, the indomitable father figure, the strong and undefeated king of the jungle. Pity the male **Tapetail**, then. This transparent jelly-like fish doesn't even live long enough to eat once it has come of age. It serves only to breed, then it dies. The female, meanwhile, goes on to develop into a Whalefish (most notable for the type that has teeth on its gills to act as a spare mouth). The male **Blanket Octopus** also lives only to breed, which it does by detaching one of its arms. The arm then crawls over to a female on its own.

At least the male **Electric Eel** doesn't die after becoming a dad – to 17,000 children. He does, however, have to make a nest for them – using his saliva.

Male/Female/Undecided?

It's common knowledge that the male **Seahorse** gives birth instead of the female, but what isn't common knowledge is that Seahorses are the ocean's great romantics. They date for several days first, swimming next to each other, holding each other's tails and dancing around strands of sea grass. Seeing as they only live a couple of years, dating for several days is a pretty long engagement.

Male Seahorses have a pouch a bit like a kangaroo's. The female lays her eggs directly into the pouch. The female **Leafy Sea Dragon** (a larger relative of the Seahorse) also uses the male as her nest, laying her eggs on his tail. After a three week pregnancy (nine weeks in the case of the Leafy Sea Dragon), during which he can barely move around to find food, the male Seahorse gives birth, releasing the live babies from his pouch. The male Leafy Sea Dragon shoots his babies off the end of his tail.

Unfortunately the romance is short-lived for sea horses, though: the belief that they mate for life is something of a myth. In fact, despite that early courtship, the female Seahorse usually loses interest in her mate

Single father - the female Seahorse lays her eggs in the male's pouch and then leaves him to bring up the babies on his own (Photo: NOAA)

pretty much as soon as she's laid her eggs in his pouch. She swims away, leaving him to do the rest on his own.

Seahorses aren't the only sea creatures where the male gives birth, but some species are neither male nor female. Or, looked at another way, they are both (scientifically they are described as hermaphroditic). The **Pseudobiceros**, for example, is a slithering flatworm that swims by rippling its body through the water. When two of them get together they have a duel over who will carry their children. Whoever loses the fight is the one that gets pregnant.

All **Sea Hares** lay eggs. In fact, each Sea Hare lays about 10 million of them a month. The eggs hatch a week later, and a month after that their babies can start laying eggs of their own too. Fortunately the Sea Hare (a slug-like gastropod named for the ear-like rhinophores on top of its head) and its eggs are on many fish's menu, otherwise the sea would be full of the eggs within a year.

Some sea creatures aren't technically hermaphroditic, but they can change sex (usually from female to male). The **Fairy Basslet**

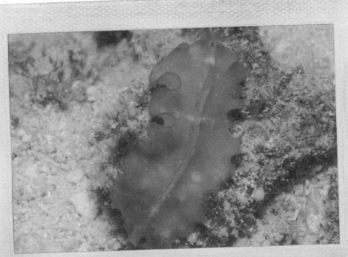

All Pseudobiceros flatworms can get pregnant, and they fight over who gets to do it - the loser is the one that has to give birth (Photo: NOAA)

is a brightly coloured fish that lives around the Great Barrier Reef. Males are territorial, and aggressive about it, and will often fight each other. Sometimes even the winner dies from his wounds. So there are generally more females than there are males, which would eventually lead to the extinction of the species. Fortunately, females can change into males. Then they start fighting too.

Something similar happens amongst various members of the Grouper Fish family, such as the **Gag Grouper**, which has suffered from overfishing in the Gulf of Mexico. Females gather in schools and if there are no males around the largest and most aggressive female becomes male. In the **Australian Saddletail Grouper** the change happens when the female reaches a certain age and size – about 39.4in (100cm), aged around 30. None of them are born male.

Various types of **Parrotfish** also school in groups that are exclusively female except for one alpha male who is basically their king, their protector, the father of all their children. If he dies, at least one of the females will change gender to replace him. Some females can also change into extra large males that are very colourful and very aggressive, almost more like generals.

With all these creatures changing from female to male, certain types of **Dragonfish** are rare in that a lonely male can become a female if it will increase his chances of finding a mate. It's not a problem he'd face if he had been born an **Ostracod**.

The Cloning of the Clones

Darwinulidae don't need men. They haven't done for about 200 million years. In that time (nearly) every member of this particular family of freshwater Ostracod has been female. It hasn't hurt their numbers. In fact, it has probably helped the species blossom. Darwinulidae clone themselves (the process is scientifically called parthenogenesis). It's actually an efficient way for a species to spread. Female Darwinulidae don't need to waste any time finding a husband, and one individual can start a whole new colony of Darwinulidae all on their own.

Three male Darwinulidae were discovered in Japan in 2006, but the whole male thing hasn't caught on. So long as the female Darwinulidae can populate the species just fine on their own, there's little point in being a boy.

Plenty of other creatures have the ability to breed with themselves too. A **Salp**, the barrel-shaped jelly-bodied victim of the Phronima (see page 45), can produce hundreds of clones of itself. Until they are big enough to go off on their own, they all link together in a chain, swimming and feeding with their identical siblings.

The female **Pacific Sea Nettle** (a jellyfish-like creature that hides behind a plant-like name) carries her eggs in her mouth. Once the young Sea Nettles are fully formed she releases them into the water, where they find a surface to attach to. Each one then clones itself several times, with the clones growing as buds on the side of the original.

In recent years marine biologists have been baffled by apparent spontaneous parthenogenesis, particularly among sharks in captivity. A female **Bonnethead** (a type of Hammerhead) living in an American zoo gave birth to a live pup in 2001, despite living in a tank with three other females, and no males. When scientists tested the baby's DNA they found she had the same as her mother's. If she had had a father she would have had some of his DNA too.

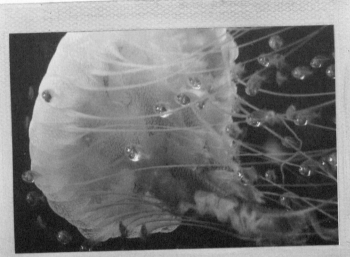

These fish look tiny in front of a Pacific Sea Nettle - it can be 3ft (1m) across, and its tentacles can be 15ft (4.6m) long (Photo: NOAA)

Though the dried-out **coral** sold by unscrupulous merchants in Far Eastern tourist shops looks crystalline, coral is not in fact a rock. It isn't a plant either. Corals are actually colonies of polyps (you can read more about what they are in the section about another such colony of polyps, the Portuguese Man of War, on page 93). All the polyps in a coral colony are separate lifeforms, but they work together to build the skeleton, and swap food with their neighbours too. Not only can they survive when separated from their friends, but polyps detached from the rest of the colony by strong currents or predators can start their own colony elsewhere.

Marine Sponges do something similar. Like coral, Sponges are animals commonly mistaken for plants because they don't move. But they're not actually stationery. Sponges are covered in flat cells called pinacocytes. A Sponge can move if the pinacocytes on one side expand while the pinacocytes on the other side contract. So it doesn't move so much as shape-shift away from its previous position, though it can only move about a fifth of an inch (4mm) a day doing this. Small pieces of

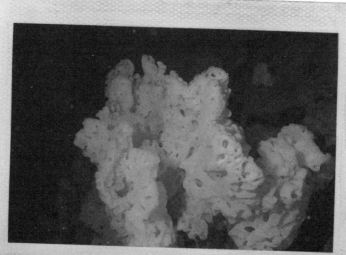

Synthetic sponges weren't invented until the 1940s - until then Marine Sponges could be used for cleaning, amongst other things (Photo: NOAA)

Sponge broken off from the rest can settle on another surface and start to regrow.

Most people know that if a **Sea Star** loses one of its rays (arms), it can grow another one, in the same way many lizards can grow another tail. However, what most people don't know is that not only can the Sea Star grow another ray, but the lost ray can grow another Sea Star too.

Not all species can do this, and it doesn't happen all the time. As with lizards losing their tails, Sea Stars often lose a ray to a predator or because they have injured it in another way, so those rays are unlikely to develop into new Sea Stars. A healthy ray that detaches from its parent Sea Star looks very odd as it develops because it is basically one fully grown Sea Star arm with several baby ones growing out of it.

If Sea Star populations dwindle then individuals can detach rays on a regular basis to boost numbers again. Of course if it only has five to begin with then it has to wait for them to regenerate. This isn't a problem for the so-called Eleven-armed Sea Star. Despite the name it often has up to 14 rays.

Like lizards, Sea Stars can detach limbs at will - unlike lizards, new Sea Stars can grow from those detached limbs (Photo: NOAA)

Though they can't clone themselves, other species share the Sea Star's regenerative abilities, notably some lobsters and crabs, such as the **Stone Crab**. Their large claws grow back in a year, so in Florida fishermen remove one claw then throw the rest of the crab back. Male **American Lobsters** sometimes lose one of their claws while arm-wrestling a rival over a potential mate. Fortunately they can regenerate them too. Unfortunately they sometimes regrow the wrong limb, so instead of developing another fighting claw they might develop a very unhelpful walking leg instead.

From Birth to Death, or Not

Often living for over 200 years, the **Giant Clam** is one of many sea creatures that make our time on the planet seem short. One was found in the Arctic that marine biologists believed to be 400 years old. Clams only move around for the first week of their life, then usually settle in one place for the rest of it. This means that Giant Clam in the Arctic was probably settling down at the time when Queen Elizabeth I was on

The Giant Clam was once nicknamed the Man-eating Clam - you'd have to hang around for a long time waiting for its shell to close on you, however (Photo: NOAA)

the throne of England and William Shakespeare was in the middle of writing his greatest works.

But even the Giant Clam dies young compared to a colony of **Black Coral** discovered off Hawaii in 2009. Scientists used carbon dating to discover the colony is nearly 4,300 years old, making it by far the oldest living organism on the planet. The first polyps started the colony in the middle of the Bronze Age, and it was already nearly a thousand years old when Tutankhamen became Pharaoh of Egypt. In the meantime it has gone through hundreds and thousands of generations of polyps.

Meanwhile the **Krill** age backwards – sort of. It's actually just a clever trick these shrimp-like crustaceans (a favourite food of everything from penguins to whales) use during the winter to help them cope with the freezing cold temperatures. Most crustaceans moult, shedding their shell as they grow bigger, but the Krill shed their shells so that they can shrink back to their childhood size. They need less food, so are better prepared to survive the winter.

An honourable mention must go here to the **Hydra**. It's a freshwater creature, a cnidarian related to the Sea Anemone, but it has mastered cloning, regeneration and ageing in a way that could teach everything else a thing or too. Like the Pacific Sea Nettle it can create clones that grow out of its side until ready to live independently. Like the Sea Cucumber it can separate parts of its body and then reform them again. And like the Sea Star it can regenerate lost body parts, and lost body parts can regenerate new Hydras.

But the Hydra takes these regenerative abilities to the next level. The Hydra can regenerate all of its cells, and in theory it can do so indefinitely. That means that while a Hydra will probably be eaten or succumb to disease at some point, there's nothing in its biology that could stop it actually living forever.

Chapter 5
MONSTERS OF THE DEEP

It's said we know more about the surface of the moon than we do the oceans. Like space, the deepest parts of the sea are dark and difficult to explore, not least because the pressure at the bottom can exceed 15,000lb (6,800kg) per square inch – that's the equivalent of having almost 200 tractors parked on top of you. Where science runs out of knowledge about space, science fiction writers pick up the baton. But some of the real creatures in the sea are beyond their imagination too.

Beware the Giants (Some of Them)

Being big might be considered an advantage against both prey and predators, but it also means you need to eat a lot more. It's no coincidence that the most successful species in the sea also tend to be the smallest – such as zooplankton (see page 94). There are billions of plankton, but only about 10,000 Blue Whales.

The **Blue Whale**'s tongue is the size of an elephant. The tongue alone weighs 6,000lb (2.7 tonnes), but that's only a small fraction of the Blue Whale's total weight of 300,000lb (136 tonnes) – about the same as an Airbus 340 jet. At a maximum length of 110ft (34m) the Blue

Whale is the largest creature ever known to have existed. Fortunately for us its throat is only as wide as a saucepan (though its major blood vessels can be as wide as a dinner plate), and it generally only eats krill and copepods.

Next to a Blue Whale the **Whale Shark** looks like a dwarf. However, it is still the biggest fish in the sea (the Blue Whale being a mammal) at lengths of up to 46ft (14m). It has a 6ft (1.8m) mouth, ideally sized for swallowing people whole, but it actually only eats plankton, and needs a mouth that big to strain sufficiently large mouthfuls of seawater to satisfy its similarly huge appetite.

Two jellyfish to avoid are the **Nomura's Jellyfish** and the **Lion's Mane Jellyfish**. Both have bells with a diameter bigger than a man – about 6–8ft (1.8–2.4m). Their tentacles can grow longer than a Boeing 737 jet – around 100–120ft (31–37m). The Lion's Mane Jellyfish has eight clusters of tentacles, each containing about 100 sticky toxic tentacles. Their venom causes pain, cramps and respiratory failure. Meanwhile the Nomura's Jellyfish plagued fishermen off Korea and Japan a few years ago, with groups of 500 or more ruining the catch by

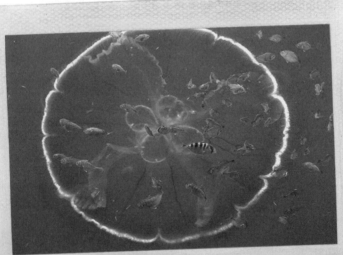

Jellyfish have no digestive, circulatory or respiratory system – they absorb everything they need through their very thin skin (Photo: NOAA)

coating it in poison and slime. The fishing industry's solution was to catch them, cook them, salt them and then market them as a tasty new novelty snack.

The **Japanese Spider Crab** is a gentle giant. From claw to claw the largest one caught was 13ft (4m) across. Undoubtedly if you were sitting on a beach and one came out of the sea you would turn and run, but the Japanese Spider Crab spends its 100-year lifetime below 160ft (50m), eating carrion and shellfish. It needs strong claws to get into shells, and it is capable of causing serious injury with them.

Superstitious sailors used to call the **Manta Ray** the Devilfish, and feared it could sink ships by seizing the anchor chain and dragging the vessel under the waves. Actually the Manta Ray is even less of a threat to us than its smaller cousin the Stingray (see page 40). It eats only plankton and fish larvae. The Manta Ray's enormous pectoral fins can be up to 25ft (7.6m) across. They look like wings, and in fact the Manta Ray can breach the surface and launch itself into the air. It doesn't do this out of aggression, but you probably don't want to be sitting in a dinghy in its way.

Gentle giants - these Japanese Spider Crab could grow to 13ft (4m) across but mainly eat plants, molluscs and small fish (Photo: Bryce Edwards)

Another creature that has a mythical reputation is the **Giant Clam**. The biggest have shells 4ft (1.2m) across and weigh 570lb (260kg). Contrary to the divers' legend, it's next to impossible for someone to get an arm or leg trapped in a Giant Clam's shell. Inside the shell the vividly coloured fleshy mantle of the Giant Clam hides, fed by dinoflagellate algae which provides it with sugars and proteins. The Giant Clam needs to open its shell so that the algae receives sunlight for photosynthesis, but the shell opens and closes so slowly a diver would run out of air long before he could get trapped by it.

Look at a photo of a **Giant Isopod** which lacks anything to gives away its size and you would probably think it's an underwater woodlouse. In a way, it is, because the purple-grey Giant Isopod is related to its land-based lookalike, and can roll itself into a ball when threatened like the woodlouse too. But it's the size of a small dog. At 16in (40cm) long, the Giant Isopod lives in Antarctica, 2,000ft (610m) down, scavenging for

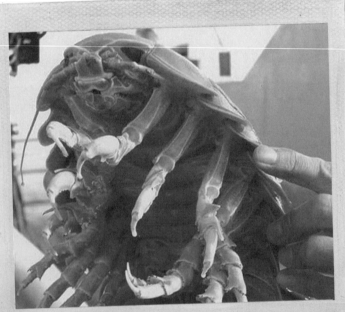

Like a giant woodlouse - the Giant Isopod can curl itself into a ball when threatened, just like its little land-based cousin (Photo: NOAA)

dead whales and squid in the mud of the seabed. Interestingly enough, it's considered a delicacy in some parts of Asia, and some people even keep them as pets.

Do Sea Serpents Exist?

On their way across the Atlantic in 1901 the crew of the Royal Navy frigate HMS *Daedalus* spotted a strange creature swimming close by. Crewmen were often prone to superstition, but even the captain later corroborated their story to *The Times* – much to the embarrassment of the British government. They certainly saw something, but their imaginations might have turned it into a sea serpent.

Several creatures fit the bill, particularly the **King of Herrings**, which isn't actually related to herrings at all. A type of Oarfish, the King looks like a long, thin, silver eel – though it can be as long as a Whale Shark. It moves through the water by undulating the reddish fin along its back. Properly known as the Regalecus Glesne, it got its common name from fishermen who saw it herding a shoal of herring and thought it was leading them rather than preparing to eat them.

It might have been a shark. Referred to as a living fossil, the **Frilled Shark** bears only a passing resemblance to its relatives. Growing to 6.6ft (2m), it is elongated and thin, and has big frilly gills (hence the name). It is also rather ugly, especially when it arcs and ripples its body as it swims – just like sea serpents are supposed to do.

However, it's worth remembering that the first stories of sea serpents didn't originate at sea, but on land. Skeletons discovered on shore seemed to suggest a dinosaur-like creature with a long thin neck was still swimming in the oceans.

Actually, such a creature is still swimming in the oceans to this day. Remove the gaping mouth and gills from a **Basking Shark** (along with the rest of its muscle and flesh) and you're left with a skeleton that looks just like a plesiosaur's, an aquatic dinosaur whose skeleton looks like a giant snake attached to a giant turtle. The Basking Shark's skull is actually quite small, but it needs a 3.3ft (1m) mouth to swallow 330,000 gallons (1.5 million litres) of water an hour to filter enough plankton to sustain its 40ft (12.2m) long body.

What About the Kraken?

Norse sagas of a thousand years ago tell of Viking voyagers falling foul of a terrible monster that normally lives at the bottom of the sea between Norway and Iceland, but which rises occasionally to pluck sailors off the decks of their ships, or to crush the ships entirely in its many tentacles.

What became known as the Kraken probably started out as a rare sighting of either a **Colossal Squid** or a **Giant Squid**. Colossal and giant might mean the same to us, but clearly as far as squid are concerned colossal means 46ft (14m) and giant means a whopping 66ft (20.1m).

The Colossal Squid has eyes the size of beachballs, but uses them to keep an eye out for predators rather than to hunt. Believe it or not, the Colossal Squid looks like lunch to some sea creatures, such as the Sperm Whale. The Colossal Squid's tentacles are armed with sharp hooks for grabbing its prey (large fish and other squid, mainly) and Sperm Whales have been caught with scars on their back caused by the Colossal Squid's hooks.

The Giant Squid's tentacles, on the other hand, are lined with suckers 2in (5cm) across, which all have small razor sharp teeth. Most of what we know about Architeuthis (as it is properly known) comes from washed up corpses. They are carnivores and eat pretty much anything,

This is not a Giant Squid - the Giant Squid is so rarely seen that nobody knows precisely how big it can grow (Photo: NOAA)

helped by having a radula in its beak – basically a tongue with teeth for tearing prey apart.

During the Second World War sailors often believed the tall tales about the Giant Squid preying on survivors floating in the water after a ship sank. This is just the 20th-century version of the Kraken myth, however. Far more likely is that the survivors were picked off by sharks, as happened after the USS Indianapolis sank.

One type of shark might also carry some responsibility for the Kraken myth prevailing in another way. The **Cookiecutter Shark** is only 1.7ft (0.5m) but it has almost 500 teeth. It doesn't look or act like any other shark. Indeed, when it attacks its prey (such as a whale) it forms a suction cup with its mouth, bites down, then swivels around to cut out a circular piece of flesh, several inches across. Such marks on whales were assumed to be damage caused by giant suckers, and giant suckers need giant tentacles, and giant tentacles need a giant monster.

As well as whales the Cookiecutter Shark has also been known to attack submarines and underwater cables, perhaps because of their electrical field (see page 80). It's not a maneater but a Cookiecutter Shark did bite a human once and took a nasty round chunk out of him – let's just say he couldn't sit down for quite a while afterwards.

Jellyfish Wars

The Nomura's Jellyfish that plagued Japanese and Korean fishermen a few years ago (see page 68) was native to their waters. Mnemiopsis Leidyi, on the other hand, is a notorious invader, which arrived in the Black Sea in the 1980s. Perhaps the locals could have learnt something from the Japanese and Korean fishermen and tried to market the new arrival as a tasty snack. After all, it already had a food-like common name they could use – the **Sea Walnut**.

The Sea Walnut was originally from the west Atlantic, where it wasn't at the top of the food chain and had plenty of predators, as well as competition for food. A type of Comb Jellyfish, the species reached the Black Sea in the ballast of ships – the ships drew in seawater containing Sea Walnuts in the west Atlantic and then released the water again in the Black Sea. There, Sea Walnuts didn't have any predators or competition, and multiplied rapidly (helped by an ability to clone themselves without a mate).

The whole ecology of the Black Sea began to change under the reign of the conquering invaders. Soon there were dozens of Sea Walnuts

A Comb Jellyfish, so-called because of the 'comb' of cilia (hair-like protuberances) that it uses to swim (Photo: NOAA)

for every square foot (hundreds for every square metre) of water. They feasted on the native crabs and fish, almost completely wiping out the native populations of anchovy and sprat. It looked like nothing could stop them.

But then something did. Ironically enough it was another type of Comb Jellyfish, and another invasive species which arrived in the Black Sea the same way the Sea Walnut did. Unlike the Sea Walnut, **Beroe Ovata** doesn't eat the kind of fish native to the Black Sea. Instead its favourite food is, conveniently enough, Sea Walnut. Supplied with all the Sea Walnut they could eat, the number of Beroe Ovata shot up. And the more Beroe Ovata there were, the more Sea Walnuts they ate. Then when Sea Walnut numbers became too few to sustain the Beroe Ovata army, the number of Beroe Ovata dropped too.

Beroe Ovata may have won the battle of the Black Sea, but its war against the Walnut is far from over. In 1999 the Sea Walnut showed up in the Caspian Sea and swiftly reduced the biomass of zooplankton by

75 per cent. In 2006 the Sea Walnut was discovered in the North Sea, and in 2008 it reached the Baltic too.

Even More to Avoid

As well as disgusting things actually in the sea, there are some pretty disgusting things floating on top or flying above it, such as the **Fulmar**. This seabird looks like every other gull until you get close enough to realise it isn't. Anyone within several feet should beware the Fulmar's beak – not because it will bite, but because it uses projectile vomit as a weapon, and it has quite a range. The Fulmar's vomit is oily, yellow, sticky and stinks of rotting fish. If it gets in other seabirds' feathers they can't get it out, so can't fly, and because they lose their buoyancy in water, can drown too.

The **Coconut Crab** doesn't live in the sea either. It does as an infant, but as soon as it comes ashore as an adult it loses the ability to breathe underwater, and can never go back. During the Second World War soldiers reported entire islands and atolls in the Pacific covered by swarms of Coconut Crabs.

Bird mess falling on your head is meant to bring good luck - but that isn't the worst thing the Fulmar can produce (Photo: NOAA)

Because it lives on land this brings the imposing Coconut Crab into frequent contact with people. Far from timid, it will happily enter people's homes, and has earned the nickname of Robber Crab because, just like a magpie, it is attracted to shiny things. Sometimes it makes off with pots and silverwear. It's probably best to just let it take whatever it wants. After all, the Coconut Crab is the largest land-living arthropod and can grow to the size of an oil drum.

It's called the Coconut Crab because its massive claws can crack a coconut shell with ease, and could probably do the same to a human skull. They can also lift weights of about 64lb (29kg). Once it has a hold of something the Coconut Crab won't let go. If that something is your head, your only hope is to tickle its undersides. Yes, really. Tickling this ticklish giant is the only way to make it open its claws.

The Coconut Crab could squash the **Soldier Crab** underfoot. But despite being a diminutive 1.4in (3.5cm) long, the Soldier Crab can send beachgoers running from the surf. It's one of those creatures that looks harmless when it's on its own – but which is rarely seen without

A ticklish monster - the best way to make this 3ft (1m) giant loosen its grip on you is to tickle its underside (Photo: John Tann)

A swarm of Soldier Crabs marching forwards - most crabs can only crawl sideways (Photo: Rob and Stephanie Levy)

hundreds or thousands of other Soldier Crabs. They march like an infantry column, searching for food, and in such numbers that they make it look like the ground itself is rippling.

Plenty of other creatures become terrifying when they swarm. The **Golden Cow-nose Ray** of Central America looks quite beautiful on its own, but when they migrate to summer feeding grounds these 7ft (2.1m) rays travel in groups (called fevers) of up to 10,000. Thousands of **Caribbean Spiny Lobsters** move together too, walking in convoy, head to tail, looking for deeper water. They keep in contact using their antennae, and if one gets sick en route the others abandon it.

It's not just the Nomura's Jellyfish (see page 68) and the Sea Walnut (see page 73) that swarm either. Every summer since the mid-1980s, swarms of the toxic jellyfish **Rhopilema Nomadica** have descended on the Mediterranean, passing through the Suez Canal from their home in the Red Sea. At their worst, these swarms can stretch 60 miles (100km) along the beaches of North Africa. Meanwhile in 2007, billions of **Mauve Stinger Jellyfish** – or in other words a 10 square mile (26km square) swarm – got into an Irish salmon farm, where they promptly ate 100,000 fish.

Most creatures that swarm have a good reason to do so, usually for protection (safety in numbers and all that). That nobody knows why the **Hammerhead Shark** swarms makes it all the more menacing when they do. Few types of shark swim in a school, but hundreds of Hammerheads all swim in the same direction, a uniform distance from each other, and turn at exactly the same time. Before the numbers of Hammerheads dwindled, these swarms would have involved thousands of them. The Hammerhead has few predators, so they're not doing it for safety, and they aren't hunting together either – at night they break away to feed alone.

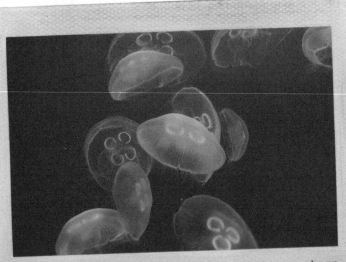

When a few poisonous jellyfish wash up on shore in Australia, beaches are closed - after all, the rest of the swarm is still in the sea (Photo: NOAA)

Chapter 6
SHARK ALERT!

Look into the face of a shark (not always recommended) and you are looking into our planet's prehistoric past. This is the closest you will get to seeing a real live dinosaur. Sharks are one of the most successful creatures in the oceans. The ancestors of modern sharks were swimming in the sea over 400 million years ago. But while dinosaurs succumbed to the changes the planet went through, sharks have changed very little in millions of years. They are the ultimate apex predator. From the age of the dinosaur to the age of man they have simply not needed to adapt.

As Richard Dreyfuss's character states in the movie version of *Jaws*, a shark is basically just an eating machine. When they're not eating, sharks are looking for something to eat, or giving birth to more little eating machines. No wonder the popular image of sharks is of a primal killer. But the popular image is wrong. Sharks are intelligent, and smart enough to be trained – brave marine biologists have managed to teach some sharks to distinguish between different shapes and colours.

For sure, the shark is an amazing animal. Of course, that's small comfort if you're being dragged underwater in the jaws of one.

A sad end for a magnificent creature - the Great White Shark is now listed as vulnerable by the International Union for the Conservation of Nature (Photo: NOAA)

A Sixth Sense

No, sharks aren't psychic. But in dark or murky waters they can't rely on their sense of sight to spot small prey. Indeed, it's far easier for a small fish to spot a shark that's several hundred times its own size, even at a distance, in unclear waters – and get out of the way, fast. Consequently many sharks rely on the element of surprise when hunting, so it's important they know where their prey is before their prey knows where they are. For this they have a sixth sense.

Dotting the underside of a shark's snout you can find a large number of tiny holes. These jelly-filled pores are called ampullae of Lorenzini, and they are what give sharks their sixth sense. Like our human ears, these cells have tiny hairs, but instead of moving when affected by sound, the hairs in the ampullae of Lorenzini react to changes in electrical fields. Everything in the sea has an electrical field. Every muscle movement, from a whale arcing its tail up and down, to the heartbeat of a tiny fish, causes a change in their electrical field.

A shark is like a radio, and the ampullae of Lorenzini are its antennae, picking up distant transmissions about lunch. Just as a radio signal gets stronger the closer you are to the transmitter, so too does the electrical signal the shark receives as it hones in on that unsuspecting fish merrily swimming along in the belief it still has a long life ahead of it.

The shark isn't the only creature with this sixth sense. The **Duck-billed Platypus** also uses a form of electroreception to hunt its prey.

As well as their sixth sense, sharks also have a super-developed sense of smell, which means they can smell dinner long before they can see it. Their hyper-sensitive nostrils can detect the tiniest of chemical traces in the water, such as faecal matter or blood. A shark can smell a single drop of blood in the sea from a quarter of a mile (0.4km) away. It can then follow that smell like a line that leads it straight to its prey. So it's probably best not to go swimming in shark-infested waters after you've cut yourself.

Man on the Menu

You are most likely to be attacked by a shark in late morning or mid-afternoon on a hot weekend in July or August while swimming in 5ft (1.5m) of water, about 50ft (15m) from the beach. But it's only statistically likely then because that's when, where and how most people go swimming in the sea.

Of the roughly 500 species of shark, only a dozen or so are any threat to us. Each year there are about 100 attacks worldwide, and of them less than ten ultimately prove fatal. Most people survive, make a full recovery, and then have a nasty scar with which to impress people. To put the statistics in context, for every single person killed by a shark off the American coast each year, about 1,000 people drown.

The three types of shark responsible for most attacks are the **Tiger Shark**, the **Bull Shark** and the infamous **Great White Shark**. But despite the media sensationalism, these 'maneaters' don't actually eat people. Contrary to the common perception, sharks don't like the taste of human meat, and usually stop after the first bite. So perhaps the quickest way to get rid of a hungry shark is just to let it have a quick nibble on you. Or maybe not.

Most people killed by sharks die from either blood loss or shock. And the rest usually drown, because both blood loss and shock can cause unconsciousness – fatal if you're swimming. Sharks tend to bite your lower legs because they're particularly vulnerable, but also bite

Lord of the ocean - the Great White Shark in its natural environment (Photo: Hermanus Backpackers)

hands and feet if you fend them off. It's rare that a shark bites any limbs clean off, but its teeth can strip the flesh from your bones, and deep wounds are common. The worst place to be bitten is your abdomen. There are no bones to protect your belly so even a shallow bite can let your intestines spill out into the sea.

If it makes you feel any better, some sharks have nictitating membranes – extra eyelids that slip down over their eyes to protect them when the shark goes in for the kill. So it's unable to see what it's about to eat in the last few seconds. If that's you, it's nothing personal.

A good way to ward off a hungry shark (well, better than letting it bite you) is to punch it hard on the nose or in the eye. Unfortunately that does depend on you seeing it coming, and unfortunately most sharks attack from behind. It's not honourable of them, but it is safer for them. You don't get to be the ultimate apex predator by giving everything else in the sea a fair chance, after all.

White Death

Carcharodon Carcharias is better known by many other names: Great White Shark, White Shark, White Pointer, as well as its bone-chilling nickname, White Death. Out of the 100 shark attacks on people every year, about half are suspected to be by the Great White. Hence the nickname.

But despite its mythological status as the most fearsome shark of them all, the Great White would much rather feast on sea mammals like seals, sea lions and whales, along with sea turtles and carrion. It is found in almost all tropical, subtropical and temperate waters, with the largest populations off Australia and the cape of South Africa. The densest population can be found around Dyer Island off the western cape, which has a channel dubbed Shark Alley because of the sheer numbers that gather there.

British tabloid newspapers got excited in 2008 when the remains of porpoises and seals washed up on beaches in East Anglia, some of them with horrific bite marks 9in (23cm) across. Of course, the story the papers ran wasn't about dead porpoises or seals, it was about a possible

The Great White Shark is infamous for its violent attacks – they can even leap entirely clear of the water (Photo: Hermanus Backpackers)

Great White Shark swimming off the coast of Norfolk and Suffolk. This, despite the fact that the Great White's bite radius can be twice that size. However, the story wasn't necessarily pure fiction. There are reliable records of Great White Sharks around the Cornish peninsula and even swimming up the Bristol Channel as late as the 1850s.

The largest Great White ever caught (off Cuba in 1945) was 21ft (6.4m), but there are unsubstantiated reports of another seen off Canada in the 1930s that was a colossal 37ft (11.3m). The Great White is born 3ft (1m) already, and as an adult can weigh in excess of 5,000lb (2,270kg). That doesn't stop it leaping clear of the water if it wants to. In short bursts the Great White can swim at speeds up to 35mph (56kmh). By comparison, American Olympic champion David Holmes Edgar has held the record for fastest human swimmer for decades, and he only reached 5.05mph (8.1kmh).

The Great White has the largest teeth of any shark, with the biggest growing to 2–3in (5–7.5cm) long. It can have about 250 of them at any one time, arranged in rows, with teeth behind teeth behind teeth. In a lifetime the Great White can get through tens of thousands of them, and loose teeth often become embedded in its prey. The bite force of a Great White has been estimated at around 18,000 Newtons – that's the equivalent to having a truck resting on top of a razor-sharp knife pointed at your belly.

Jaws – the True Story

Much of the Great White Shark's reputation today can be blamed on *Jaws*, both Peter Benchley's bestselling novel and Steven Spielberg's blockbusting movie adaptation. But the spate of real shark attacks in July 1916 that partly inspired Benchley to begin with probably didn't involve a Great White at all. Experts now believe another of the three so-called maneaters, the **Bull Shark**, was responsible instead.

Usually found in coastal areas of warm oceans, the fearless and fearsome 11ft (3.4m) Bull Shark is almost unique among sharks in that it can survive in freshwater, not just the saltwater of the sea. This means it can (and does) swim up rivers and streams (as long as they are deep enough) and enter lakes. People have lost limbs and been killed by Bull Sharks in the Karun River in Iran – 250 miles (400km) from the sea. There have been reports of Bull Sharks spotted in the Mississippi River as far north as Illinois. Bull Sharks have even been found in the Amazon, 2,000 miles (3,200km) from the sea. Meanwhile after the

The Sand Tiger Shark - sometimes they swallow their own teeth to help 'recycle' the minerals in them (Photo: Dimo Dimov)

floods that hit north-east Australia in 2011 two Bull Sharks were seen swimming near a McDonalds in Queensland.

In July 1916, while war-torn Europe descended into the hell of the Battle of the Somme, neutral America enjoyed a lovely start to the summer season. A heatwave in the north-east attracted thousands of people to the beaches of New Jersey on the holiday weekend before Independence Day. One of those was 25-year-old Charles Vansant, on holiday with his family, who went swimming before dinner on 1st July. Nobody rushed to help him when he started screaming. Eyewitnesses thought he was just shouting at a dog. When a lifeguard finally pulled Vansant from the water everyone saw the flesh was stripped from his leg. He bled to death before help arrived. The lifeguard later revealed he saw the shark that did it – it followed him and Vansant into the shallows, as if hoping for a second bite.

Over the next couple of weeks four more people were attacked along the Jersey Shore. Five days after Charles Vansant died, 27-year-old Charles Bruder was also attacked while swimming. A shark severed his legs and bit him on the abdomen. Lifeguards hurried to his rescue, but Bruder bled to death before they even got him up on to the beach.

One shark attack would have been cause for concern. Two attacks in the same area within days of each other became a national headline, prompting panic and hysteria all along the Atlantic seaboard. Mass shark hunts took place. Rewards of $100 were offered to anyone who caught the shark. The net result of all this was a massive upswing in the number of supposed shark sightings. Most amounted to nothing. It was reasonably easy for people to dismiss reports of a shark in Matawan Creek, especially as the creek is 16 miles (25.7km) inland.

On 12th July, 11-year-old Lester Stillwell and his friends were playing in the creek when they saw what they thought was a large log drifting through the water toward them. By the time the boys saw the dorsal fin rise out of the water it was too late. As the boys scrambled out of the creek the shark lunged for Lester Stillwell, seized hold of him and dragged him underwater.

Meanwhile Stillwell's friends ran and called for help. One of those who responded was 24-year-old Watson Fisher. Along with several others he dived into the creek, but as he reached the boy's body the shark attacked again. This time it seized Fisher, sinking its teeth into his right thigh. Horrified onlookers saw everything. They gave up on Stillwell's body, but dragged Fisher to safety. But it was too late for him too. He died from blood loss later that afternoon.

Less than half an hour later, and only half a mile away, another boy was also attacked by a shark. It grabbed 14-year-old Joseph Dunn by the leg and would have dragged him to his death too. Fortunately Dunn's brother and another friend also grabbed hold of him. After a remarkable tug-of-war with the shark (that's the story the boys told, anyway), they managed to wrestle the teenager away from the jaws of death. In doing so they saved his life. Of the five people attacked over two weeks, Joseph Dunn was the only one to survive.

It's still not known whether the Jersey Shore and Matawan Creek attacks were carried out by one particularly bloodthirsty shark, or whether the attacks were unconnected and an unlikely coincidence. No single shark was caught that could be blamed for any of them, anyway. The attacks just stopped after Dunn's lucky escape.

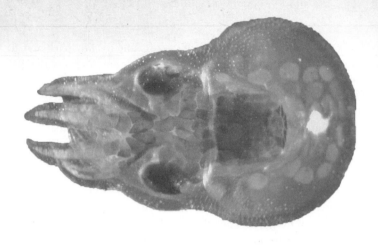

Chapter 7
THE BEST OF THE REST OF THE WORST

After reading this book you might never want to dip a toe in the sea again. But *How to Snog a Hagfish!* only really scratches the surface. Beneath the surface there are 230,000 different species, and that's just counting the ones we already know about. Marine biologists are discovering new creatures all the time, especially in the deepest parts of the oceans, where being disgusting is pretty much expected of you.

Some disgusting things have so far avoided being featured in the book, but there's just enough room to squeeze in the best of the rest of the worst.

Us

There was no avoiding this one forever. One of the most disgusting things in the sea, on the sea, indeed anywhere near the sea is **mankind**. As an invasive species we are far worse than the Sea Walnut (see page 73). No other creature comes close to having such a detrimental effect on the delicate ecology of the oceans. In June 2011 the International Programme on the State of the Ocean (IPSO) released a report and their findings were catastrophic – that, unchecked, our actions will ultimately lead to a mass extinction event. From over-fishing to climate change to pollution, we are putting pressures on the marine environment that sea creatures won't be able to survive.

The statistics are so bad it might be tempting to admit defeat and say the problem is just too big to solve in time. Five million tonnes of oil ends up in the sea every year, but only 5 per cent of that comes from oil spills like *Deepwater Horizon*. Some 92 million gallons (418 million litres) enters the oceans as rain suffused with car exhaust fumes. Though deliberate dumping of toxic chemicals in the oceans was banned in 1996, that hasn't stopped tens of thousands of tonnes of lead and mercury ending up in the sea each year. These chemicals don't go away quickly. Pregnant women are often still advised not to eat tuna or salmon because they may contain mercury.

Our use of fertiliser on land is having a catastrophic effect on the oceans. Eventually the chemicals leach through the soil and end up in rivers, which carry them into the sea. There they continue to do what they did ashore – stimulate plant growth. The nutrients, nitrates and

The most disgusting thing in the sea strikes again - 5 million tonnes of oil ends up in the oceans every year, one way or another (Photo: NOAA)

ammonia in fertilisers cause a rapid and unnatural bloom in algae and phytoplankton (see page 94). These suck up all the oxygen, depriving all other sea creatures. The process is called eutrophication, and it has created so-called 'dead zones' – areas where nothing but algae and phytoplankton lives. There are now about 400 of these dead zones worldwide, the largest covering over 8,000 square miles (nearly 21,000 square km). That's about the size of Wales.

In Chesapeake Bay near Washington DC oysters used to eat up all the excess chemicals. Nature could have sorted itself out, but then man interfered. Over-fishing reduced oyster numbers so they could no longer prevent eutrophication. The Potomac River that feeds into Chesapeake Bay is also home to male Bass that have started laying eggs because of the amount of human hormonal medicines in the water. We have to realise that everything we use can and probably will end up in the sea eventually.

In 1997 an American yachtsman sailing across the Pacific came across a patch of floating rubbish so big it took him a week to plough through it. It became known as the Great Pacific Garbage Patch and nobody knows how big it really is. Estimates suggest there could be about 90 million tonnes (99.2 million tons) of floating rubbish, most of it plastic that won't disintegrate for decades. It will just continue to float around the Pacific like an island of landfill. In 2010 a similar patch was discovered in the North Atlantic too.

Meanwhile governments around the world are still looking to the oceans to provide a safe place to dump nuclear waste. Bury it at the bottom of a trench a few miles (or kilometres) down and it can't possibly affect us up here on the surface – or so the thinking goes. Not much thought is given to the creatures that live down there, clearly.

A lot of talk about tackling climate change involves reducing carbon emissions because as a greenhouse gas too much carbon dioxide in the atmosphere will lead to the planet heating up. But the effect excess carbon has on the oceans is far more catastrophic, and it is already happening. Increased levels of carbon dioxide have made the sea more acidic. This is causing many species problems with things as fundamental as growing shells and bone development. Nothing demonstrates this better than coral – in parts of the Pacific 80 per cent of coral has now gone.

So what can be done? Fortunately it's not too late to stop things getting worse, even if not all the damage can be reversed. But it will take the concerted efforts of governments (all of them), businesses, and individuals (all of us) to make fundamental changes to the way we live and treat the planet. That's easier said than done, but as the evidence for climate change grows increasingly undeniable, the motivation is also growing.

On a side note, it's worth mentioning that our species could also go into Chapter 2. Some of our eating habits, particularly when it comes to seafood, are truly disgusting, and also very cruel. In both China and Japan shrimp are eaten alive, served in alcohol so that they are easier to stab with a fork. You have to chew quickly to kill it. In Korea they serve a dish called Sannakji Hoe – a live octopus whose arms are still furling and unfurling when you cut into it. But the worst is the Japanese dish Ikizukuri. In a restaurant you pick your own fish, which is then filleted alive and served on a plate with its heart still beating. Sometimes it can even be put back in the tank to recover before the second course.

The Rest of the Worst

Plants on land are often limited as to how big they can grow by the amount of water they can extract from the soil. Of course, this isn't a problem in the sea. To the east of Bermuda, in the part of the Atlantic called the Sargasso Sea, the waters are so calm that a thick layer of brown seaweed covers the surface like a carpet at times. It's a great place for turtles and eels to spawn, which they do in their millions. A less hospitable type of seaweed is **Caulerpa**, dubbed the 'killer algae'. A toxic invader, its 200 poisonous fronds grow to 9ft (3m) long and kill fish and other plants.

Growing at 3ft (1m) a day, fronds of the tree-like **Macrocystis** can rapidly reach 200ft (60m) – taller than most trees on land. Also known as Giant Sea Kelp, Macrocystis is actually a type of algae. Usually many Macrocystis specimens grow together, anchored to rocks on the seabed with suckers rather than roots. In cool shallow waters entire forests of this seaweed can develop, with the fronds reaching toward the surface, and the sunlight it needs for photosynthesis.

Just like the rainforests on land, forests of Macrocystis are home to a wide variety of sea creatures, some of which are hunting (or conversely, hiding from) each other. Sea Stars and crustaceans live at the bottom, while sharks and even the Grey Whale can be found at higher levels. Some experts have suggested that these Macrocystis forests also helped the first colonisation of America – ancient fishing communities could

It's a jungle down there - established forests of Giant Sea Kelp can grow at a rate of 3ft (1m) a day (Photo: NOAA)

have followed the forests from Asia during the last Ice Age, using the Macrocystis as a buffer against rough seas, and also as a source of food en route.

Sea Snot is the popular name for Sea Mucus but, despite the name, Sea Snot isn't what comes out of a whale's blowhole when it sneezes. Sea Snot forms from clusters of what is called 'marine snow'. This includes dead matter floating through the oceans that sticks to other dead matter, as well as microscopic creatures (and sometimes also shrimp and other larger crustaceans too) either caught up in the growing mass or trying to feed on it. It looks like a dirty yellow-brown blob of slime.

Sea Snot occurs naturally in the Mediterranean, where slower-moving warm water helps the stuff to accumulate. As the planet heats up and sea temperatures rise the growth of Sea Snot has accelerated, and because winters are warmer too, these accumulations are lasting longer each year. Some of them grow so big they can form a field of mucilage some 124 miles (200km) long.

Divers have also reported swimming down to depths of 50ft (15m) and, in lowlight conditions, not seeing a huge mass of Sea Snot before swimming into it. Sea Snot can be potentially dangerous. It can harbour bacteria and viruses like e.coli which are harmful to sea creatures (and us, if we swallow infected water). If it gets into their gills Sea Snot can also suffocate fish, and if it sinks to the seafloor it can smother everything that lives down there.

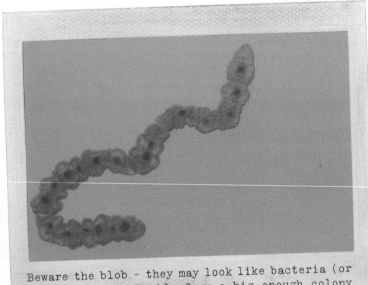

Beware the blob - they may look like bacteria (or eggs) but when Zooids form a big enough colony they can smother sea life (Photo: Christopher Laumer)

Not to be mistaken for Sea Snot, **Zooids** can also look like a blob of slime. Indeed, a colony of Zooids (because they consist of many tiny creatures, not one large one) is sometimes nicknamed 'the blob'. A yellow-cream colour, looking a bit like scrambled eggs, Zooids can also smother other sea creatures. They form a mat-like covering that can overwhelm mussel and clam beds and coat dock installations.

CREATURE FEATURE
The Portuguese Man of War

The polyps that make up the Portuguese Man of War are also types of Zooids. Four different types make a Man of War. The most obvious is the transparent or at least translucent inflated cyst that floats on the surface. The cyst can grow to 6in (15cm) and it provides the Man of War with buoyancy. As the Man of War has no means of self-propulsion the cyst also acts like a sail, catching the wind and allowing the Man of War to drift wherever the breeze takes it. Of course, without the ability to change direction, the Man of War is also at the mercy of currents and tides, which is why the Man of War is not uncommonly found washed up on a beach. If threatened by a predator on the surface (or above it), the Man of War can let the air out of the cyst and submerge to safety.

Beneath the surface the Man of War has tentacles that can grow up to 165ft (50m) long when uncoiled. These tentacles are another polyp in the colony. They contain stinging nematocysts, and drift through the water, fishing for prey. When a small fish falls foul of the Man of War's venom, the tentacles can coil back up, dragging the prey within reach of the polyps that do nothing but eat. The fourth polyp is reproductive. The Man of War is another creature that can effectively clone itself (see page 61).

The Man of War usually travels in a group with 1,000 or more others, which probably explains why beaches in southern England were closed in 2008 after only a few washed up. Each year in Australia the Man of War is responsible for 10,000 stings. Its venom is not usually lethal to humans unless they are allergic, but can leave painful marks for several days. The important thing to remember if stung is that the Portuguese Man of War is not a jellyfish, and using vinegar to treat stings (see page 38) will actually make them worse!

The Most Important Species on the Planet

Every mouthful of seawater contains hundreds of thousands of tiny organisms called plankton. In fact, half of the biomass in the oceans consists of plankton. What this means is that if you took every living thing in the ocean and liquidised them into one big soup, half of that soup would consist just of plankton.

A bowlful of Zooplankton - some of these tiny crustaceans are the larvae of much bigger sea creatures (Photo: NOAA)

Plankton is the all-encompassing general word for thousands of different species. They can be divided into two different sorts: **phytoplankton**, which are tiny plants, and **zooplankton**, which are tiny animals. Zooplankton includes tiny crustaceans, little fish and the larvae of bigger creatures. Phytoplankton are like plants on land, making their own food using energy from sunlight (photosynthesis). Two trillion tonnes of the stuff grows in the oceans every year.

Pretty much everything in the sea either eats plankton or eats something that eats plankton, which makes it the most important species in the oceans. However, plankton is far more important than that. Phytoplankton produces more than half the planet's oxygen. By comparison, the Amazon Rainforest is sometimes called the planet's lungs, but it only produces a fifth of the planet's oxygen.

So that mouthful of water you accidentally swallow might be full of tiny living things, but they won't do you any harm. In fact, without them, the entire human race probably couldn't survive.

Plankton may be the most important to us, but many of the creatures in this book play important roles in the ecology of the sea – from Parrotfish creating sandy beaches to coprophage Blennies and necrophage Cusk Eels keeping the waters clean, not to forget oysters and jellyfish doing their bit to sort out the mess we've made. Yes, the creatures in *How to Snog a Hagfish!* may look disgusting or do disgusting things, but actually, they're all pretty amazing, when you think about it.

INDEX OF DISGUSTING THINGS